HOW TO HELP YOUR CHILD WITH HOMEWORK

Every caring parent's guide to encouraging good study habits and ending the Homework Wars

For parents of children ages 6-13

by Marguerite C. Radencich, Ph.D.
and
Jeanne Shay Schumm, Ph.D.

Edited by Pamela Espeland

free Spirit
PUBLISHING

Library of Congress Cataloging-in-Publication Data

Radencich, Marguerite C., 1952-
    How to help your child with homework:
    Bibliography: p.
    Includes index.
    Summary: every caring parent's guide to encouraging good study habits and ending the Homework Wars: for parents of children ages 6-13 / Marguerite C. Radencich and Jeanne Shay Schumm.
    p. cm.
    1. Homework. 2. Education—Parent participation. I. Schumm, Jeanne Shay, 1947- . II. Title.
LB1048.R33 1988
371.3'028'13—dc 19   88-19019
                            CIP

ISBN 0-915793-12-1 (pbk.):

10 9 8 7 6 5 4 3 2

Printed in the United States of America

Cover and book design by MacLean & Tuminelly

Cover and text illustrations by Caroline Price

Free Spirit Publishing Inc.
123 N. Third Street, Suite 716
Minneapolis, MN 55401
(612) 338-2068

DEDICATION

To John and Jerry

CONTENTS

Introduction

"I didn't do my homework because you forgot to remind me."

"I didn't do my homework because my parents came home late from work."

"I couldn't do my homework because I had a swollen finger."

"I did my homework but I left it on the bus."

"I did my homework but it was stolen from my locker."

"I did my homework but my baby sister wrecked it."

"I did my homework but the dog ate it."

"I left my homework in my pocket and my mom put my jeans in the wash."

Teachers have heard excuses like these since the first teacher made the first homework assignment. And as long as they keep giving homework, students will keep trying to get out of doing it.

So why do teachers bother? Why do they continue to inflict homework on kids, their parents, and themselves? Actually, there are several excellent reasons.

- ▶ Homework encourages children to practice skills they haven't yet fully learned.

- ▶ Homework gives children opportunities to review skills they might otherwise forget.

- ▶ Homework enriches and broadens a child's knowledge.

- ▶ Homework teaches responsibility.

- ▶ Homework allows for tasks which are too time-consuming to be finished during school hours.

As a parent, you can probably think of a few more reasons yourself. You may remember times from your own childhood when a homework assignment made the difference between fully understanding a subject or barely grasping it, between excelling on a test and just scraping by. There may have been occasions when you actually *enjoyed* doing your homework — when you sat at the kitchen table or sprawled on the living-room floor, working at your own pace on a project that fascinated you, without the distractions of the classroom.

Because we are teachers and tutors, we have often been asked by our friends, relatives, neighbors, and the parents of our students for advice on handling the homework issue. (One of us has also been on the other side, having brought up a child through public and private schools.) Because we are researchers, we have tried to find answers. We spoke with other educators and came away with ideas and suggestions. We spoke with parents to discover what they had tried and what had been successful for them.

For many parents engaged in the Homework Wars, the obvious strategy is to look back at their own experiences as children and draw from them. Unfortunately, this seldom produces workable solutions. Schools today are different than they were back then. Recent decades have seen dramatic changes in family makeup, in the pressures being put on kids to succeed at earlier ages, and in the way school subjects are taught.

Just as some of our parents suffered when the "new math" was introduced during the 1960's, parents today are frustrated as we watch our children quickly surpass our own computer literacy. We're confused by the modern approach to mastering writing skills, which requires children to correct grammar and punctuation errors only on revisions and not on first drafts. We feel out of touch with the changes in curriculum and the burgeoning amounts of information our children are given to learn. We wonder if we can keep up.

Regardless of what parents know or don't know (or think they don't know), most are still eminently capable of helping their children with homework. You don't have to be an expert in every subject. You don't have to be up-to-date on the latest teaching methods. All you have to be is caring, concerned, and willing to spend some time with your child (or children).

We're not talking about hours every day from now through high school graduation. This book stresses the teaching of *study skills*, which children don't always learn in school. As yours learn them from you, they will, in effect, be learning how to learn on their own. We predict that the more time you spend teaching these skills today, the less you'll have to spend in the future — and the more independent your children will become.

Homework doesn't have to be unpleasant. It *shouldn't* be unpleasant. It may not be as much fun as playing or watching TV, but there's no rule that says it has to be pure, unrelieved torture. At the very least, it ought to be bearable, for you as well as your child. This book offers specific strategies, tips, and techniques that can make homework more bearable — and even enjoyable — for everyone concerned. They have worked for other families, and they can work for you.

Recent educational research has shown that *when parents become involved in their children's schoolwork, children do better in school.* They become more effective learners, and they become more willing learners. By deciding to help your child with homework, you will do more than end the Homework Wars. You will give your child the tools he or she needs to succeed.

Marguerite C. Radencich
Jeanne Shay Schumm

November 1988

1
Getting Started

"A child is the only known substance from which a responsible adult can be made."
— Unknown

Deciding who should help

Many parents feel that they don't have the skills to help their children with homework. In fact, research has shown that the *quality* of the parent-child interaction is more important than the actual techniques used. You might be surprised at what a good teacher you can be!

But helping with homework doesn't have to be solely your responsibility as a parent. You may discover that more than one family member is willing and able to lend a hand.

As you decide who should help your child with homework, consider these questions:

▶ Is there someone in your family who's a "natural teacher"? Maybe it's a parent. Or maybe it's a sibling or other relative who lives nearby and is willing to help.

▶ Is there someone in your family who's especially knowledgeable about or talented in a particular subject area? Maybe Dad studied French in college. Maybe big sister is a math whiz.

You might also look beyond your immediate family. If your child spends the after-school hours with a sitter, perhaps she (or he) can help. Or maybe the sitter you regularly call for weekday or weekend evenings can assist. And don't forget about other children your child knows. Kids who study with friends can help each other. One of our sisters studied for years with a neighbor.

For the sake of simplicity, this book is written to the parent and assumes that the parent is the one who will most likely be involved. But that doesn't have to be the case. Ask around; you may find help from other sources.

Of course, you should exercise good judgment in any of these arrangements. Make sure that the person really wants to help and understands this basic principle: *Homework should NEVER be done FOR the child*. Also make sure that he or she has the time. Helping with homework should not put an excessive burden on anyone, particularly siblings. If big brother has an especially busy school and social schedule, the added responsibility may not be beneficial to him or to the child in need of assistance.

Setting a schedule

Children (and adults) respond well to structure and consistency. We all feel more secure when we know what to expect. (If you need convincing, think back to how you felt on your child's first day of kindergarten, compared to how you feel now when he or she leaves for school in the morning.)

This sense of security is the main reason for setting a firm schedule for homework sessions. Another equally valid reason is that it eliminates one of the most common battles in the Homework Wars: arguing about when to do it. Finally, it ensures that it *will* get done by a reasonable hour. Many children are natural procrastinators. If we let them, they'll put off starting their homework until the last possible minute — or they won't do it at all.

You may be blessed with a child who does homework without prodding or reminding. If this is the case, the child should be allowed to set his or her own schedule, with only occasional monitoring from you.

However, it's far more likely that you will need to get directly involved in this process. In deciding when your child's homework sessions should be scheduled, keep these guidelines in mind:

> ▶ Most kids need some time to unwind after school and before settling in to do their homework. Yet they shouldn't wait until it's so late that they're too tired to complete it effectively.

▶ Children have trouble concentrating when they're hungry. If home-work must be done before dinner, offer a healthy snack. (Sugary snacks or soft drinks containing caffeine are NOT recommended.)

▶ Younger children have a harder time sitting still for extended periods than older children. Fortunately, short study sessions often lead to more learning than longer ones. For example, it's better to practice flashcards for two 10-minute sessions than one 20-minute marathon.

Most families already have their own schedules — times when people arrive home from school and work, times when they sit down to dinner, times when the kids go to sports or scouts. Although it will almost certainly be a challenge, try to fit homework in where it will be least disruptive. On the other hand, it should be a priority, and it should be taken seriously. We can't tell you the best place to fit it in because we don't know your family's situation. But we *can* reassure you that once you set a schedule and stick to it, it *does* get easier. And once your child gets used to the idea that he or she WILL DO HOMEWORK, no matter what, you can afford to be flexible when the need arises.

There may be one problem that needs addressing in advance: the problem of what we call the Overprogrammed Child. Parents naturally want their children to have everything. However, the child who has karate classes on Mondays, piano lessons on Tuesdays and Thursdays, and scouts on Wednesdays may simply be doing too much.

Kids need time for homework and chores, and they also need free time for play. If your child is involved in a variety of activities, you may want to reassess the situation — especially if his or her grades are suffering, or there are signs of emerging emotional difficulties. A few to watch for include:

▶ refusing to go to school or talk about school,

▶ refusing to do homework, and/or

▶ physical ailments with no identifiable medical cause.

If your child evidences any of these, or if you have other reasons to believe that your child may be overprogrammed, then one or more of these extracur-ricular activities should be stopped.

After you have determined a specific time (or times) for homework sessions, you're ready for the next step: determining how that time should be orga-nized. Here are some parent-tested recommendations:

▶ Encourage your child to start each homework session by looking over everything that needs to be done. Ask, "Which parts can you do on your own? And which will you need help with?"

▶ Suggest that your child do the most difficult or distasteful task *first*, before fatigue sets in. There's nothing worse than having your child ask you to explain a complicated math problem when both of you are ready to call it a day.

▶ When homework involves memorizing information or reviewing for a test, this should be done early in the session, while both you and your child are fresh. Then, at the end of the session, go over the material one more time. If possible, you may want to review it again in the morning before school.

Homework Schedule

PREPARED FOR: Johnny   PREPARED BY: M♥M (xoxo)

4:00–4:30   After school play time.
4:30–5:30   Start homework. FIRST, figure out what you need to do. NEXT, decide which things you want me to help you with. (Do HARDEST homework first!)
5:30–6:00   Stop homework. Play time.
6:00–7:00   Dinner.
7:00–7:30   Finish any leftover homework.
7:30–8:30   Play or TV time (IF HOMEWORK IS DONE). Check with me BEFORE turning on the TV!
8:30   Bedtime.

HELP!

"I get home from work just in time to fix dinner. My daughter has gymnastics after school and eats dinner as soon as she gets home. Both of us are exhausted afterward. How can we possibly fit homework in?"

Your case is an exception to our "do-the-hardest-homework-first" rule. You may want to try letting your daughter do her easiest homework in the evening, before bedtime. Then, depending on how much homework she has, have her get up half an hour earlier in the morning, dress and eat breakfast, and complete the more difficult work before leaving for school.

"My son does his homework as long as there isn't anything interesting on TV. If there is, I have to nag him to do it."

What's wrong with exercising some parental control? Decide on a specific number of hours per day (preferably one at the most) during which your son is allowed to watch television. Have him tell you which programs he wants to watch, and either give your approval or suggest something else. And make it a rule that if he really wants to watch his programs, he has to finish his homework first. He will probably scream and yell and argue, but stand firm; once he learns that you mean business, he'll settle down — and buckle down.

"My son does his daily assignments without any problem. But he always wants to stay home on days when reports or special projects are due."

He needs help budgeting time for long-term assignments. Start by doing some "backwards planning." Use a calendar and count back from the day a project is due to determine how much time he has. Then work together on a "project plan." For suggestions, see pages 102 - 104.

Setting up a home study center

One of us grew up with three brothers and sisters. Everyone had a special place for doing homework. One claimed the dining room table, another retreated to our parents' study, and the other two worked in their bedrooms.

Deciding *where* your child should do homework is as important as deciding *when* it should be done. Learning styles differ from child to child, and the study center should allow for these differences. Some points to consider include:

▶ **Lighting**

Good lighting is always important, but some children prefer brighter lights than others. Any child with his or her own desk should have a desk lamp.

▶ **Seating**

Good posture helps concentration. This isn't to say that your child can't slump into a beanbag chair to read a story, but for optimum attention to homework, a straight-backed chair at a table or desk is best.

▶ **Noise**

Although some children can study in the midst of TVs and radios blaring, other children playing, dogs barking, and parents conversing, it's better if the study center is relatively quiet. If possible, it should be located away from where distracting toys are kept. A "Do Not Disturb" sign can add a nice touch.

▶ **Materials**

Often the first few minutes of homework time are wasted as children search the house for materials they need. You can put an end to this by stocking the home study center with writing instruments, erasers, paper, notecards, paper clips, pencil sharpeners, White-Out, and other supplies. Make a small chalkboard or slate available for exercises that would normally be done on scratch paper, and hang a bulletin board for posting calendars, important notices, and directions for special projects.

▶ **References**

The study center should include a small reference library. For children in first grade, we suggest a "pictionary"; for children above first grade level, supply a dictionary written at a level your child can understand. (Good elementary dictionaries include the Ginn, Macmillan, and Scott, Foresman series.) There are even thesauruses written for children. A set of encyclopedias saves trips to the library; the *World Book* is an excellent resource for older elementary school children, since it's easier to read than most other encyclopedias. An atlas and a globe can also be useful.

▶ **Your presence**

Generally speaking, the younger the child, the more likely it is that he or she will get down to work if you are nearby. You shouldn't have to hover over your child during every minute of every homework session, but if he or she is at the kitchen table while you're preparing dinner, or at the dining-room table while you're reading the newspaper in the next room, the opportunities for distraction will be fewer. And you'll be around to answer questions and provide encouragement. Older children with a proven track record of doing their homework without constant supervision can be allowed to study in their rooms or another place of their choosing, as long as it meets the criteria outlined above.

Homework and home computers

Many parents have asked us whether it's a good idea for their children to use a computer when doing homework. Our answer is: It depends.

Clearly it's important for children to be comfortable around computers and to know what computers can do — in short, to become computer literate. Making a computer available in the home is an excellent way to facilitate this. But be prepared to exercise some parental control! Excessive use of computers is as bad as too much TV. Children who are always in front of computer monitors don't have time for socializing, reading, or exercise.

If you already own a computer, consider letting your child use it *occasionally*, not constantly, and provide appropriate software. There are many programs available today that can enliven repetitious drill-and-practice in math, reading, and spelling. See pages 114 - 117 for suggestions.

These may not necessarily help with Tuesday night's homework, but they may sharpen your child's skills in the required areas. And that's a benefit for the long term.

Some of the more creative programs on the market also build critical thinking and problem-solving skills, another long-term benefit. Children who learn to think will learn to draw on this ability on many different occasions. Recommended programs and publishers include:

▶ For grades K-6: *Gertrude's Secrets, Gertrude's Puzzles*, and *Moptown Parade*. For science problem-solving in grades 4-9: *Rocky's Boots*. Write: The Learning Company, 4370 Alpine Road, Portola Valley, CA 94025. (Apple, IBM, Commodore 64)

▶ For grades 2-12: *The Pond*. For grades 4-12: *Color Keys* and *The Factory*. Write: Sunburst Communications, 39 Washington Ave., Pleasantville, NY 10570-9971. (Apple)

Another valuable use for computers is word processing. But before a child can successfully use a word processor, he or she must first learn how to type, or "keyboard." Some inexpensive programs that teach keyboarding include:

▶ *Typing Tutor IV.* An upgrade of *Typing Tutor III*, a program that sold 300,000 copies in three years, *IV* tailors lessons for each user. Its "Letter Invaders" game spices up practice. Write: Simon & Schuster Software, Gulf & Western Building, One Gulf + Western Plaza, New York, NY 10023. (Apple, IBM, Commodore 64)

▶ *Master Type.* Eighteen lessons show fingers resting at the "home" position, then wiggling to demonstrate how to move to the upper and lower rows of the keyboard and back. Write: Mindscape, 3444 Dundee Rd., Northbrook, IL 60062. (Apple, IBM, Commodore 64)

▶ *Mavis Beacon Teaches Typing.* "Speaks" in conversational tones while analyzing typing mistakes. Users can type in jokes, riddles, and rhymes. The program also displays a keyboard with fingers that type along with the user, and a built-in metronome encourages even typing. Includes an "Indy Racer" game. Write: Electronic Arts, 1820 Gateway Drive, San Mateo, CA 94404. (IBM)

Although all children should learn to compose with a pencil, word processing programs can greatly simplify tasks ranging from vocabulary sentences to book reports. They make it easy to insert or delete sentences, reorganize paragraphs, and correct spelling; many programs include built-in "spellcheckers" and thesauruses.

CAUTION

Check with your child's teacher *before* giving your child permission to do writing assignments on the computer. Some teachers prefer that assignments be handwritten, and younger children especially need practice in this skill. Most teachers prefer that children *not* use spellcheckers.

Whether a child can successfully use a word processing program may depend on how sophisticated the program is. Some software manufacturers have developed programs that are extremely simple to use, and a few have even targeted programs to children. Recommended programs include:

▶ *Snoopy Writer.* This simple and inexpensive program allows children in grades 1-6 to write, edit, and print. Write: Random House Media, 210 East 50th St., New York, NY 10022. (Apple)

▶ *StreetWriter Plus.* This more complex (and more expensive) program is designed for grades 3 and up. Write: Broderbund, 17 Paul Drive, San Rafael, CA 94903. (Apple, IBM)

Computers can also be used to gather information for research projects or reports. When equipped with a special device called a *modem* and connected to your telephone, a computer can call up on-line databases containing newspaper, magazine, and even encyclopedia articles. In addition, a modem can provide access to local "bulletin boards," some of which may have computer programs that can be downloaded, or copied, for home use.

▶ To find out about databases, visit your local library and talk to the computer specialist or database coordinator. Explain that you're looking for a good source of general information and ask for recommendations. It may be that your library subscribes to one or more databases and can demonstrate their use for you.

▶ To find out about bulletin boards in your area, check with the media center specialist at your child's school. Or contact local computer Users' Groups. (If you don't know where to start looking for these, ask at a store that sells the type of computer you have at home.)

CAUTION

While many bulletin boards may be accessed for free, most databases charge by the minute. If using a database also requires a long-distance telephone connection, the costs can add up quickly!

What if you *don't* already own a home computer? Should you consider buying one? If you can afford one, it would probably be a good investment, especially if your child is using computers in school. You may want to purchase a computer that's identical to or compatible with the kind the school has chosen. Check with your child's teacher or the school media center specialist for specifics.

If you decide to go this route, you should plan on buying the following equipment:

▶ the computer itself (with at least 64K internal memory; again, check with your child's teacher),

▶ a keyboard (if one isn't attached to the computer),

▶ a monitor (although some computers can be hooked up to your television set),

▶ one or two software programs, and

▶ a box of blank disks.

You may be able to obtain free programs from your child's school. Check with the media center specialist.

▶ Optional, but recommended, is a printer, especially if your child will want to print out assignments at home.

The two-way street between home and school

It goes without saying that the better your relationship is with your child's teacher and school, the more successful your child's school experience will be. Because homework is part of your child's school experience, it's wise to make that relationship a two-way street. Following are some suggestions for accomplishing this:

▶ **Talk to your child about school.**

Ask him or her to tell you about what happens during the day. What does your child like best about school? What does he or she like least about it? The more you know, the more prepared you will be should problems arise.

▶ **Plan to meet with your child's teacher at least three times during the year.**

Communicate your willingness to cooperate with him or her. Don't wait for a personal invitation; an Open House (most schools hold them annually) is an excellent opportunity to have a *brief* conversation. If you need more time, make an appointment.

▶ **Find out how you will be informed about your child's progress.**

Will children bring papers home on a weekly basis? Will there be interim reports between report cards? Many schools provide parents with written summaries of the curriculum. Periodically reviewing these can help you to stay informed about what your child is being taught.

▶ **If you have any cause to suspect that a problem exists, make an appointment immediately and tell the teacher why you want to meet.**

Don't just show up unannounced. Spur-of-the-moment conferences translate into incomplete information. They aren't fair to you, the teacher, or your child.

Sometimes a teacher will notice a problem before the parents do. Typically, a teacher will initiate communication with a note sent home with the child. Be sure to respond, either with a phone call or with a note of your own. Depending on the nature of the problem, you may want to schedule a conference to discuss it.

If your child is having difficulties doing school work, make sure that there are no hidden physical causes. A visit to your pediatrician, ophthalmologist, or audiologist can uncover any that might exist.

How much homework is enough?

How can you tell if your child is getting the right amount of homework? First, it helps to understand that homework policies differ widely from school to school and from state to state. Typically, the amount of homework increases as the child moves up to higher grades.

▶ **If your child consistently tells you that he or she has no homework or has "done it on the bus," check with the teacher.**

If what your child is saying is true, the teacher might be willing to assign more homework or more difficult homework.

▶ **If your child's homework load allows no time for play, check with the teacher.**

The homework load might be excessive. Discuss this possibility with the teacher and try to work out a solution together.

Between these two extremes, it's difficult to ascertain what constitutes an "appropriate" homework load. Some children will take longer than others to complete assignments. And the homework load may be heavier or lighter at certain times of the year.

In our opinion, appropriate averages are 30 minutes of homework a day for first graders and 90 minutes a day for sixth graders, with proportional amounts assigned to the grades between. Some educators recommend more, while others feel that the school day is long enough and any amount of homework is too much. If you are in total disagreement with the policy followed by your child's teacher, schedule a conference and try to reach a compromise.

How can you tell if the content of your child's homework is appropriate? A good rule of thumb is: *Homework should not involve anything that is brand-new to the child.* If your child consistently requires a lot of help with homework, schedule a conference with the teacher. Possible problems may include:

▶ Your child may not be paying attention in class.

▶ Your child may have a listening or memory problem and may not be learning what is taught in class.

▶ Your child may be using homework as a way to get your attention.

▶ Your child's teacher may be assigning work which has not yet been taught.

▶ The assignments may be unclear, unfair, or without purpose.

Once you identify the problem, you and the teacher can work together toward a solution. Keep in mind that most teachers really *want* to help their students. If you maintain a positive attitude, most problems can be solved at the classroom level.

HELP!

"My daughter's teacher insists that she copy sentences on notebook paper instead of filling in the blanks on the workbook pages. It takes her forever to do this. As a taxpayer, aren't I entitled to have my daughter write in the workbook?"

Students who only fill in blanks or write the correct letter for an answer (in multiple-choice exercises) do not learn how to form sentences. Your teacher may believe that your daughter needs more practice in this area.

There may also be a financial motivation for this procedure: The more workbooks the school purchases, the less money is available for other materials such as library books.

In either case, your daughter's teacher is acting reasonably. If the amount of work is excessive for her, or if your daughter has a special problem, a conference with the teacher should help. If the problem is more than laziness on your daughter's part, the teacher may consider cutting down on the size of the assignment. If this isn't possible, try having your daughter do some of her homework in the evenings and complete it in the mornings before going to school.

"My son usually understands his homework, but he finishes it too quickly and makes many errors."

Check his homework before allowing him to leave his study center, and have *him* make the necessary corrections. Limit your help to general suggestions for improvement. Examples: "You've forgotten two periods. Find where they belong." Or: "Five of your math problems are wrong. Check your answers."

Another alternative is to block off a homework period. If your son finishes his homework before the end of the period, let him fill the rest of the time with schoolwork-related activities you give to him.

Finally, a reward system for neat and accurate work may be in order.

"My daughter's teacher refuses to give her reading workbook pages to do at home, even though my daughter is perfectly willing to do them. The teacher tells me that reading library books is better for my daughter than workbook pages. Is this true?"

The teacher is right on target. Children who spend a lot of time on workbook pages often don't see the relationship between these pages and reading books. Because reading series used in schools have limited vocabulary, limited sentence difficulty and length, and limited story type and length, it's critical that your daughter be exposed to *real* books as often as possible. If you need help deciding which ones she should read, ask your school librarian or the children's librarian at your local library for suggestions.

TWENTY TIPS
FOR HOMEWORK HELPERS

1. **Maintain two-way communication with your child.**

    Don't just lecture. Listen and respond to what your child has to say. When you respond, don't plead or argue. (Pleading puts your child in charge; arguing creates a no-win situation.) Instead, respond assertively and positively.

2. **Don't give your child a choice unless you mean it.**

Instead of saying, "Would you like to work on your science homework now?", say, "It's time to work on your science homework. Please join me at the table." Or, if you really want to offer a choice between two tasks, phrase it in a way that's likely to get the desired response. Example: "You can either do your science homework now or after dinner. But if you wait until after dinner, you won't be able to watch your favorite TV program."

3. **Set goals with, not for, your child. Then focus on one at a time.**

Start with one that your child is almost guaranteed to achieve. That will make the others more appealing, and continued success more likely.

4. **Expect progress.**

We all respond to the expectations other people have of us. (It's the self-fulfilling prophecy syndrome.) If your expectations are low, your child's achievements are likely to match them. If your expectations are high, *but not unreasonable*, your child will respond in kind.

5. **Make your child aware of his or her improvement. Reward achievement.**

Don't "pay" for every accomplishment with a treat or a promise. Often it's enough simply to say, "You did a really good job on that map. I'm proud of you." But if your child works especially hard on a difficult assignment and completes it successfully, that's worth celebrating.

6. **Praise generously, yet honestly.**

Praise will lose its effectiveness if used indiscriminately. And a child can usually tell when you're not being sincere.

7. **Direct praise to the task at hand.**

Saying "You spelled 8 out of 10 words right. Much better!" is more specific than "Good for you!" Specific praise guides future behavior.

8. **Try not to show disappointment if your child doesn't do as well as you'd like.**

Look for your child's strengths. Avoid criticism. The child whose performance is poor doesn't need reminding; he or she needs encouragement and reassurance that you value him or her *regardless of performance*.

9. **Be enthusiastic. Use humor.**

   Starting every homework session with the "Star Wars" theme might be going overboard. But it doesn't hurt to smile and say, "I like spending this time with you." And you don't have to be deadly serious about it. Laughter, shared jokes, and even a tickle or two can go a long way toward lightening the homework load.

10. **Use timers and competition judiciously.**

    For some children, a timer spurs effort and puts an end to stalling; for others, a timer is anxiety-producing. If the latter seems true for your child, put it away. Some children enjoy competing against themselves and trying to better their past achievements, and if this is the case with your child, that's fine. But competition with friends, brothers, or sisters can be threatening and debilitating, especially if the child is at an academic disadvantage.

11. **Be prepared to teach.**

    Even though the teacher is responsible for teaching the subject matter, this doesn't always happen. You may need to "fill in the blanks." Skimming the textbook and carefully reading lesson materials and handouts will prepare you for this role.

12. **Use concrete materials rather than abstract ones, especially (but not exclusively) when working with a young child.**

    For example, it's easier to learn "2 + 3" with blocks than with pictures. And it's easier to learn with pictures than with numbers.

13. **Help your child build associations between what he or she already knows and what is being learned.**

    Children learn new concepts by learning how they are like and different from concepts they already know. For example, "Multiplying fractions is like regular multiplying except...." "A stream is like the canal behind our house except...." Or: "The electrons in an atom circle the proton. What circles the sun?" A child who envisions the solar system has a better understanding of what goes on in an atom.

14. **Provide adequate practice.**

    Children shouldn't just learn material; they should actually *overlearn* it to promote the development of long-term memory. Try to ignore complaints of "We already did that! This is BORING!" But don't run a subject or a concept into the ground. Know when to stop.

15. **Provide variety. Take breaks.**

   If a child starts fidgeting excessively over a math book, switch to spelling for a while. Return to math later. In between, share a snack, take a short walk, or have a joke-telling session.

16. **Encourage creativity.**

   Although you do have to be careful about "sticking to the rules," a certain amount of creativity can "help the medicine go down." A story in one of the basal readers (reading books) tells of a child whose Thanksgiving homework assignment was to make a Pilgrim doll. The child's mother was an Eastern European immigrant. The child dressed a doll in Russian attire, and the doll served as a lesson to the class that the U.S. has had many kinds of pilgrims over the years.

17. **Encourage independence.**

   For example, if your child is able to read directions independently, encourage him or her to do so.

18. **Take every opportunity to build your child's self-esteem.**

   This includes, but isn't confined to, most of the other tips already outlined here. Use your imagination and your natural affection and concern to think of other ways to show your child that he or she is a worthwhile and important person.

19. **Check with the teacher BEFORE correcting your child's homework.**

   Many teachers want to see a student's mistakes. They use them to determine where more teaching is called for. A perfect parent-corrected paper can be misleading and can rob a child of the extra help he or she may need.

20. **Show a positive attitude toward school.**

   If you have problems with your child's school or teacher, *don't* discuss them with the child. Instead, show your respect for school by emphasizing the importance of regular attendance, a neat appearance, and grades that reflect your child's true capabilities. Then make an appointment to speak privately with the teacher.

2

Troubleshooting

"You cannot put the same shoe
on every foot."
— Publius Syrus

What to do when you have difficulties working with your child

Experience has already shown you that parenting isn't easy. Whenever you make a change in the way you relate to your child, you can expect problems to surface somewhere along the way.

Deciding to help with homework is making a change in the way you relate to your child. He or she may resist your help at first — or accept it initially and resist it later. Your best-laid plans may founder on the realities of temper tantrums and power struggles.

What can you do if you have difficulties working with your child? First, you can resist the temptation to assume that any and all homework-related problems are the fault of your child, the teacher, or the school. A surprising number may trace back to your own expectations and behaviors.

There's nothing unusual about this; even parents aren't perfect. The point is that these problems *can* be solved. All it takes is willingness on your part to examine your expectations and behaviors and modify those that get in the way.

Start by reminding yourself of these simple truths: You are an adult; your child is still a child. You have years of experience to draw on; your child is relatively new to the world. You are capable of problem-solving, analyzing, and reasoning; your child may not yet have developed these skills. Finally, your child is counting on you to be older and wiser, to set rules and boundaries, and to offer guidance when and where it's needed. Often the more a child rebels and resists, the more that child is crying out for parents to take charge. When you say, "You WILL do your homework, and that's final," you're not being "mean" or "unfair" — you're being a parent! And the more firm and consistent you are, the easier it will become and the more responsive your child will be.

In talking with parents about difficulties they have had in working with their children, the following issues have come up again and again. Exploring them here may help you to avoid them or deal with them effectively should they arise.

▶ *"My parents never had trouble getting me to do my homework. I can't understand why my child is so stubborn about it."*

Are you treating your child the way your parents treated you? There are two simple reasons why this may be backfiring: You aren't your parents, and your child isn't you.

Even though most parents vow that they will never treat their children as their parents treated them, research has shown that we tend to repeat our parents' behaviors. It's perfectly fine to draw on the wisdom you gained from your mother and father; just be sure to leave room for your own good sense and instincts. And keep an open mind to what today's experts are saying about how children learn. Much of this information was unavailable to our parents, and we can all stand to benefit from it. For suggestions, see pages 131 - 134.

▶ *"I don't have any trouble working with other people's children. Why is it so hard with mine?"*

Many parents can do a good job teaching children — as long as they're not their own. There are many reasons for this. To begin with, you're usually not as emotionally attached to other people's children. Your expectations aren't as high. Your ego isn't as involved.

When working with your own child, you may find it hard to maintain a balance between being interested and being pushy. We all want to encourage our children to do their best. It's an almost irresistible parental urge. But it's far more effective to be genuinely *interested* in what they are doing, what they are experiencing, what they are feeling, and what their needs are. Being interested means putting them first, listening to what they have to say, and tailoring your responses to what's best for them.

You may discover that your emotions interfere with your teaching. While honesty is usually the best policy, there are times when it's best to conceal your true feelings for the sake of your child's self-esteem. For example, no child functions well in the face of parental disappointment or anger. Rather than show these feelings, take a break. Go off by yourself to cool down, or do something fun with your child. You'll both feel better.

Take time to examine your goals for your child. Do you see your child as an extension of yourself? Do you see your child as a reflection of your parenting abilities? Do you want your child to achieve everything you didn't or couldn't achieve when you were in school? Are you subconsciously trying to "keep up with the Joneses" through your child's accomplishments? Remember that your child is a unique individual — one of a kind, and one in a million. The more you project this attitude, the more your child may achieve. The freedom to be oneself is a powerful motivator.

▶ *"I must have gone over this material a thousand times! WHY can't my child get it?"*

Many parents have said to us, "I don't know how you do it. I'd never have the patience to be a teacher." So you didn't become a teacher — and here you are, forced to teach anyway. If it's any consolation, even the best teachers get impatient. As long as you recognize your impatience and are able to deal with it, don't let it concern you. It's normal, it's natural, it's inevitable!

The only time to worry is when your lack of patience — or your emotional involvement, or your expectations, or your ego — seriously hampers your ability to help your child. If it becomes clear to you that you're *not* the best person for the job, then find someone else. Many parents hire professional tutors for their children. (For more about that, see pages 28 - 29.)

▶ *"I work crazy hours and can't always supervise my child's homework."*

If your child needs homework supervision and no one is available to provide it in your place, you will need to resort to the telephone. We know of one case where a father shocked his son by checking up on him from Mexico!

How to help your child keep track of assignments

All homework starts life as an assignment, given by a teacher to a child. Unfortunately, many assignments get lost, misplaced, or misunderstood somewhere between school and home.

Unless you live in the Bermuda Triangle, there's really no reason why assignments can't arrive home in the same condition they left school. All it takes is a few new habits — and a few useful organization tools.

▶ **A bookbag**

A bookbag is an absolute must where homework is concerned. You child's should be prepared every night before school and left in a convenient, regular place for pickup in the morning.

Shopping for a bookbag can be an enjoyable parent-child outing. As much as possible, respect your child's wishes where style is concerned; certain bookbags may be "in" at school, while other are definitely "out." An unpopular bookbag stands an excellent chance of "disappearing."

▶ **Notebooks**

Children should have notebooks which facilitate organization. Large looseleaf binders with subject separators, envelopes for loose papers, and pencil cases can encourage a child to keep supplies and assignments in order. It's harder to lose or forget a looseleaf binder than a series of thin individual folders.

Again, let your child participate in the buying decision. Many children love to pick out their own notebooks and pencil cases, put things neatly where they belong, and show off their new acquisitions to their friends.

Shopping for supplies can also be an opportunity to add any "extras" to your child's home study center. A stapler, a tape dispenser, a paper punch, and a ruler can all be purchased fairly inexpensively. Label them with your child's name and declare them "hands-off" to the rest of the family. Little touches like these mean a lot to a child.

▶ **A calendar**

Many looseleaf binders come equipped with school-year (or all-year) calendars. If your child's doesn't, you may want to consider purchasing a teacher's planning calendar (available in school and office supplies stores) for recording short-term and long-term assignments. This can be inserted in the front of your child's looseleaf binder, with assignment due dates circled.

▶ **Assignment sheets**

Your child's teacher may provide these. If not, feel free to make several photocopies of the sample assignment sheets found on pages 139 and 141. Slip these into your child's looseleaf binder just ahead of the calendar, then make sure that they're kept up to date.

And there you have it — instant organization!

"My son's bookbag and notebook are a mess! Papers are stuffed everywhere and he can never find a thing."

Bookbags and notebooks can become portable trash bins. Your son needs help organizing his. After the first major clean-up (done with your assistance), require that he start each evening study session with a five-minute "tidy time." Supervise, but don't do it for him. Eventually he'll form the habit and organize his materials on his own.

"My daughter forgets her homework on purpose so she won't have to do it."

Your course of action will depend on the reason your daughter is "forgetting" her homework. Here are some possible causes and some solutions for you to try.

1. She is looking for attention.

Even "negative attention" — including displeasure and scoldings — qualifies as attention. Skip the scenes and calmly let her know that you will work with her if she brings her homework home, but you will pay little attention to her if she doesn't. Then follow through! When she does start "remembering" her homework (which she will), give her the positive attention you promised.

2. The homework is too difficult for her.

Confer with the teacher to determine whether your daughter is capable of handling the assignments. If she isn't, try to find out why. Is she having trouble paying attention in class or grasping new concepts? Does she need extra help? Does she simply lack self-confidence? Let the teacher make suggestions about what to do, and come up with some of your own. For example: Maybe your daughter needs to be shown that — with a minimum of help — she can do assignments which she had thought were too difficult. Or maybe she can be given easier assignments until she's ready to handle more difficult ones. Or maybe the assignments can be broken up into smaller, more manageable pieces.

3. Your daughter does not recognize the importance of homework assignments.

Quite often, children don't understand *why* homework is assigned or *how* doing homework (or not doing it) affects their grades. Arrange for a three-way meeting with your daughter, her teacher, and you. Ask the teacher to explain the purpose for homework in his or her class, how it is scored, and how it factors into the final grade.

4. Your daughter is just plain lazy.

It's not very flattering, but it may be true. Start by requiring your daughter to record all of her assignments on an assignment sheet. Ask the teacher to initial the sheet daily to show that an assignment has been made, and also to initial it whenever homework is handed in. Insist on seeing the sheet every evening. (You may want to tie this to a privilege or two. For example; no sheet, no TV. Or no sheet, no after-school bike rides.)

Whenever your daughter neglects to bring home the materials needed to complete an assignment, give her an alternate homework assignment or an uninteresting chore to do. Or you may try a tactic that some parents have reported as successful for them: Collect her incomplete homework on Fridays and have her spend time over the weekend finishing it. When homework starts seriously interfering with play, most children will see the light.

"My daughter NEVER brings home handouts. As a result, we never know about PTA meetings or other school functions until it's too late. And if she is given a worksheet to complete at home, it never arrives and she receives a zero on the assignment. Anything that's distributed in class is lost forever!"

This is a common problem. It's amazing how children can sort through the various handouts they receive in class and manage to bring home *only* those that have to do with field trips.

Encourage your daughter to put *all* handouts in her looseleaf notebook as soon as they are given out in class. Emphasize that she is *not* to stuff them in her desk or locker, the Black Holes of the grade-school set.

Post a chart on the refrigerator. Every time your daughter brings home a handout (whether an announcement or a worksheet), give her a star, a check-mark, or a sticker. Reward her once a certain number has been reached.

Or you might give your daughter a "special folder" just for handouts. Let her decorate it with crayons, markers, or stickers. Ask to see the folder every evening.

As a last resort, send your daughter's teacher several self-addressed, stamped envelopes to be used for mailing handouts home. This may seem like capitulation, but there's a catch: Have your daughter pay for the postage out of her allowance. This is almost guaranteed to get fast results!

"My son keeps track of daily assignments, but not the long-term ones. We just found out that he has a big assignment due tomorrow, and there's no way he can get it done without a lot of help from us."

Don't give it to him. Don't take him to the library or (even worse) offer to do the work yourself. After all, it's not *your* assignment. Tell him in a matter-of-fact way that he's simply going to have to accept the consequences of not getting it done.

Then show him how to fill out an assignment sheet and a calendar so he'll be better prepared next time. Monitor his assignment sheets until his track record improves.

How to help your child prepare for tests

Schools do not typically teach children how to study for tests. Some children manage well regardless, but others need step-by-step guidance. Here are some guidelines you can use to help your child prepare for tests, eliminate night-before panics, and lessen test anxiety:

▶ **Before the test:**

- On the day the test is announced (and provided that your child tells you about it), work with your child to plan a study schedule which does not leave everything for the last minute.

- Encourage your child to study "actively." Children who underline key words in the text (if this is allowed), take notes, and write outlines while reading are more likely to do well than those who merely let their eyes gaze down the page.

- Have your child invent questions that seem likely to appear on the test. Then have your child try to answer the questions. This will point out areas of study that need more attention and review.

- Teach your child the "STAR" test-taking strategy. (This is particularly useful for timed tests, although it can also be applied to untimed tests.)

    1. **Survey** the test to see which items can be answered quickly.

    2. **Take** time to read the directions carefully.

    3. **Answer** the questions you can answer quickly, leaving difficult items for last.

    4. **Reread** the questions and your answers, making any needed corrections.

- Reassure your child that it's okay to leave answers blank or guess answers if he or she doesn't know them or can't figure them out. Some children are reluctant to go on to the next question; they get "stuck" midway and their grades suffer as a result. Your child may need to practice this on untimed tests before attempting it on timed tests.

- Make sure that your child is well-rested and fed on the morning of the test. If time allows, you may want to take your child out to breakfast so he or she will have pleasant associations with the day.

▶ **After the test:**

- Talk to your child about the test. Which parts were easy? Which parts were difficult?

- When the graded test is handed back, work with your child to analyze any errors. Try to determine why each error was made. Was it a careless mistake? Was information omitted when your child was studying for the test? Did your child simply forget something covered during the study session?

- File the test and any notes or outlines made prior to it. These can be valuable references and study tools for later cumulative tests.

For more information on helping your child prepare for tests, see pages 88 - 90.

HELP!

"My daughter either doesn't study for tests or informs me of a test at 9 p.m. the night before — right when she's supposed to go to bed."

Teach her how to complete an assignment sheet, with descriptions of assignments (including tests) and due dates. Go over the sheet with her on a weekly basis and use it to plan study time. Use the "Before the test" guidelines on pages 23 - 24 to help her form new study habits.

"My son crams for tests the night before and does moderately well, but he forgets the material before final exams."

First, he shouldn't be cramming — he should be studying well in advance of each test. Second, it's clear that your son needs to periodically review material he has already learned. Go over past tests with him. Look back at former worksheets, papers, and reports. He needs to understand that learning is a *process,* not a series of individual units to be memorized now and discarded later.

To bribe, or not to bribe?

Teachers talk a lot about "behavior modification," "rewarding children for appropriate behavior," and "withholding rewards" (or meting out punishments) for inappropriate behavior. These may sound like new descriptions of the age-old practice known as bribery.

Should you bribe your child to do homework? The answer is yes — and no.

We all respond to bribery. Few adults would show up at work if they weren't paid to do so. Most of us trust that certain of our actions will lead to expected rewards, be they *personal* (feeling good about ourselves), *social* (being thanked or praised by others), or *material* (receiving a concrete reward). Similarly, we realize that other actions will lead to less pleasant personal, social, or material consequences.

Children's actions should also lead to consequences that are clearly spelled out ahead of time. When you set consequences, make sure that *you* can live with them! In setting consequences, what you're really doing is giving your child a choice. If your child chooses the consequence for *not* doing homework, then that consequence must be delivered with no anger, pleading, or hesitation on your part.

Most children aren't mature enough to value personal rewards, so they need more tangible external motivation. It's preferable that this take the form of social rather than material rewards (or punishments). But if the only motivation a child will respond to is material, then you shouldn't hesitate to use it. Just remember to gradually phase it out when it is no longer needed.

Children who are hard to motivate require frequent rewards. For this to have the desired effect, it's important that the rewards be *consistent* and appropriate to whatever it is you want the child to do. (Of course, any punishments should meet these same criteria.) Buying your child an expensive toy for completing an assignment is *not* an appropriate reward. Grounding your child for a month for failing to complete an assignment is *not* an appropriate punishment.

We recommend small rewards for achieving short-term goals, and equally small punishments for not achieving them. For example: a colorful sticker or a quarter for doing an assignment, or the withholding of a privilege for not doing it. Wait until later to set long-term goals (and equivalent rewards and punishments).

Whether you are using short-term or long-term goals, you may want to use a contract to formalize the arrangement. Have your child design one by himself or herself.

"My son finds any number of excuses to leave his homework. As a result, it often takes him all evening to do an assignment that should take 30 minutes. I have lectured him, and I have praised him when he's been at least moderately attentive. But neither of these approaches seems to work."

Try providing him with concrete rewards for completing his homework within a reasonable amount of time. For example, if he enjoys skateboarding, you can use this as a reward. Since you don't want to give him an excuse to fail, make your initial requirements fairly easy to satisfy. Let him skateboard for half an hour after finishing half of his homework. Later in the evening, when the other half is done, allow him extended skateboarding time.

"My daughter does her homework, but only when I scold her. How can I elimi- nate the need for constant scolding?"

You can decide to *stop* scolding — effective immediately. And you can end an ongoing power struggle that isn't very satisfying for you or your daughter.

You may think that when you scold your daughter and she does her home- work, you're the winner of the power struggle. In fact, you're the loser. Your daughter has figured out precisely how much "pushing" it takes to send you over the edge into anger. When you react to her "pushing" by scolding, you are effectively letting her control the situation.

Remember that *you're the adult* — you're supposed to be smarter and stronger than she is. You can choose to ignore her "pushing" and focus calmly on the task at hand. Figure out a reward that would mean something to her, and use it to provoke the response you want to see.

For example, if your daughter enjoys going to the movies on the weekend, tell her that she can — as long as she does her homework. Allow some room for failure until this new pattern has been established. Let her know that if she completes three out of four days of homework assignments, you'll give her the money for a movie ticket. Later you can increase that to four days out of four.

What to do when you disagree with a teacher about homework

You feel that your child is being assigned too much homework or too little, or homework that's too hard or too easy, or homework that takes too much or not enough time to complete.

Whenever you're dissatisfied with or uncertain about any aspect of your child's education, these are the steps to take:

1. Make an appointment to confer with your child's teacher.

2. Prepare for your conference by making a list of your questions or concerns. Write them down.

3. Present your questions or concerns to the teacher, then *listen to what the teacher says* in response. Don't hesitate to ask for explanations of any terms or language you don't understand.

4. If you're still dissatisfied when the conference is over, go home and think about it. (This also gives the teacher time to think about the problem and come up with solutions or strategies that may not have occurred to him or her during your meeting.)

5. If the problems persist, make an appointment to confer with the school principal. Follow the same procedure recommended for the teacher conference: Make a list of points you want to cover, then present them at the conference.

For most problems, there is no need to go any further than this in the school hierarchy. For the rare circumstance that does require intervention at a higher level, consult your local Board of Education representative.

We can't overemphasize the importance of starting with your child's teacher. This is the person who knows your child best and spends the most time with him or her. While it may be tempting to go straight to the principal, you should always give the teacher the first chance to respond.

When to hire a tutor

If your child is having difficulty doing homework or other schoolwork, and if for whatever reason you are unable to provide sufficient help yourself, you should consider seeking professional help in the form of a tutor.

Here are some of the circumstances that might lead you to take this step:

▶ Your child's teacher or the school counselor recommends it.

▶ Homework sessions with your child are frequently unpleasant or stressful.

▶ The rest of your family is suffering adverse effects because of excessive time spent with one child's homework. (A second child who wants more attention can develop learning problems as a way to get it.)

▶ Your job hours vary and you're unable to set up a consistent schedule for your child's homework.

▶ Your child's school problems are severe enough to warrant expert outside assistance.

If the problem appears to be one of attitude rather than ability, you may want to see a counselor first. But if there seem to be both academic and attitudinal causes, it's time to look for a tutor.

Your child's school system may provide free tutorial services. Start by checking out this option. Otherwise, school administrators may be able to recommend tutors known to them or suggested by other parents or teachers.

If you do decide to hire a tutor, begin with an in-person interview. Don't make your choice solely on the basis of a telephone conversation. Make sure that both of you understand and agree to the following terms and expectations:

1. If the tutoring will take place in your home, you will resist the urge to "pitch in." You can talk to the tutor briefly before each session begins and after it is over, but stay away while it's going on.

2. You will be considerate of the tutor's time. If an after-session conference runs half an hour or longer, you will offer to pay the tutor accordingly.

3. You will make every effort to provide an environment free from distractions — including bouncy dogs, overheard telephone conversations, curious siblings, and other interruptions.

4. If the tutoring will take place outside your home, you will have your child at the appointed place regularly and on time. In case of a necessary cancellation, you will inform the tutor ahead of time.

5. The tutor and you will agree upon (and put in writing) specific goals to be worked toward with your child. Progress toward these goals will be the primary criterion you will use in determining whether the tutor's services are satisfactory — and whether you will continue using and paying for them.

Before the tutor starts working with your child, set up a meeting between you, the tutor, and your child's teacher. This will help the tutor to become oriented to the teacher's routines and expectations. Afterward, the tutor should keep in touch with the teacher.

Once the tutoring begins, don't expect miracles overnight. In fact, you should be suspicious of tutors who promise such miracles. Too often, parents who hire tutors in April are disappointed when their children are held back a grade in June. Some children may require tutoring for extended periods of time.

Finally, tutoring should not cause further anxiety. It's normal for a child to be somewhat anxious during the first session. But if anxiety persists after the first few sessions, stop the tutoring. Look for another tutor and try again, or schedule a teacher conference to explore other options.

What to do when all else fails

Some children absolutely refuse to do their homework despite rewards, punishments, promises, or threats, and despite the best and most caring efforts of parents, teachers, tutors, and other concerned persons.

If your child's problems are so severe that they resist any and all of the troubleshooting strategies outlined in this chapter, you will need further professional assistance. Ask the teacher about the school's procedures for a psychological evaluation, or seek outside testing. Discuss the results in a conference with the teacher, the school counselor, and the principal.

A change in class assignment may be called for. Some children thrive when they are moved to another room at the same grade level; others need more specialized help in the form of a class for learning disabilities. Or the test results may show that a child is being underchallenged and would benefit from a program for gifted students. Or they may indicate the need for a period of psychological counseling.

Try to be objective when studying the alternatives presented to you. Keep in mind your primary purpose: helping your child. With that as your goal, you're certain to make the right decision.

3

How To Help Your
Child With Reading

*"Whoever forms a reading habit will never
lose it. It is a treasure no one can take from
him. It contains wealth that neither poverty,
nor old age, nor misery can tarnish. Thieves
cannot steal it nor storms destroy it and, like
vintage wine, it can only improve with age."*
— Arthur Langlie

How to help your child
read words

Learning to read is the key to all learning. Appalling numbers of American students are graduating from high school functionally illiterate, unable to read job applications or simple instructions. As a caring parent, there are few responsibilities you should take as seriously as making sure that your child learns to read. And if your child also learns to *enjoy* reading — something you can communicate through your own attitudes and behaviors — that's even better.

Basic to learning to read is learning how to decode individual words. This chapter provides you with strategies, tips, and techniques you can use to help your child develop this essential skill.

Teaching new words

▶ Some English words are best learned by sight, as they have no sound-symbol regularity. Examples are *the* and *one*.

▶ Other words can be taught by analogy. If your child can read the word *pet*, then you can help him or her discover that *met* and *set* follow the same pattern. Similarly, recognizing *pet* can lead to an understanding of how to read *pen* and *peg*.

▶ Despite what you may have learned yourself, it is not always wise to teach new words by encouraging your child to "sound them out." Some children will not learn to read this way. Also, since consonant sounds cannot really be pronounced in isolation, *pet* becomes *puh-e-tuh*, a gross distortion of the original word.

Nevertheless, you should be familiar with the names teachers give to the basic vowel sounds.

BASIC VOWEL SOUNDS

long **a** — as in **name**	short **a** — as in **pan**
long **e** — as in **Pete**	short **e** — as in **met**
long **i** — as in **ice**	short **i** — as in **pin**
long **o** — as in **oak**	short **o** — as in **lock**
long **u** — as in **flute** or **use**	short **u** — as in **cub**

▶ Be careful about telling your child to "look for the little words inside the big words." This can lead to words like *prepare* turning into *prep* and *are*.

Teaching prefixes and suffixes

By the end of the primary school years, children are reading multisyllabic words. If they are to become rapid readers, they must learn to recognize frequently occurring prefixes, suffixes, and roots. This is the way most adults tackle unknown words.

For example, an adult reading *microorganism* might recognize the prefix *micro* as meaning "very small," the root *organ* as meaning "alive," and the suffix *ism* as indicating that the word is a noun. For fun, test your own facility on the longest word in the English language (and you thought it was *antidisestablishmentarianism*):

PNEUMOULTRAMICROSCOPICSILICOVOLCANOCONIOSIS

Try to decipher this *before* checking your dictionary!

When teaching your child prefixes and suffixes, work on only a few at a time. Since it is easier to teach prefixes than suffixes (their meanings are more concrete), focus on prefixes first.

▶ The most effective approach is to teach each prefix in the context of several words. (For example, teach *dis-* in *disagree*, *disappear*, and *disobey*.) Be sure that the words you choose are good examples of the prefix. (For example, for teaching *in-* as the opposite of *out-*, *inside* is a good example while *incorrect* is not.)

▶ Present each new word in a sentence pair which focuses on its meaning. (For example, "I agree with you. She *disagrees* with you.")

PREFIXES

Prefix	Meaning	Examples
bi-	two	bicycle, binoculars
dis-	not	disagree, disappear, disobey
ex-	out of	exit, expel
in-	into	inside, infiltrate
in-	not	incorrect, insincere
mis-	wrong	misspell, mistake
pre-	before	prefix, precede
post-	after	postwar, posterior
re-	again; anew	reread, rewrite
re-	back	return, retreat
sub-	under	submarine, subway
super-	above; over	superman, superior
trans-	across	transportation, transition
tri-	three	tricycle, triangle
un-	not	unhappy, untrue

When teaching your child suffixes, it is usually enough that your child learn to recognize the pronunciation of the chunks (for example, *-tion* = "shun"), and that he or she be able to tell whether the suffix indicates a noun, verb, adjective, or adverb. Only suffixes with clear meanings (for example, *-ess* = woman, *-ful* = full, *-less* = without) should be taught to elementary school children, using the steps outlined on page 33 for teaching prefixes.

SUFFIXES

Nouns

Suffix	*Examples*
-al	removal, approval
-ance	clearance, importance
-ence	absence, presence
-ity	stupidity, curiosity
-ment	excitement, argument
-ness	fairness, craziness
-sion	division, explosion
-tion	multiplication, addition, subtraction

Nouns which refer to persons

Suffix	*Examples*
-ant	servant, giant
-ent	student, president
-er	farmer, teacher, dancer
-ess	waitress, actress
-ist	artist, cartoonist
-or	actor, sailor

Verbs

Suffix	*Examples*
-en	strengthen, weaken
-ify	beautify, glorify
-ize	summarize, capitalize

(continued on next page)

Adjectives

Suffix	*Examples*
-able	movable, drinkable
-al	musical, choral
-ent	present, absent
-ful	careful, thoughtful
-ic	artistic, gigantic
-ive	creative, active
-less	careless, thoughtless
-ly	sadly, truly
-ous	curious, religious
-y	curly, shiny, leafy

Adverbs

Suffix	*Examples*
-ally	naturally, totally
-ly	slowly, quickly

For lists of prefixes, suffixes, roots, and other reading-related lists, see *The Reading Teacher's Book of Lists* by Edward B. Fry, Jacqueline K. Polk, and Dona Fountoukidis (Englewood Cliffs, NJ: Prentice Hall, 1984).

Pacing your teaching

How many words should you attempt to teach during a single session? That will depend on:

▶ how difficult the words are,

▶ how old your child is,

▶ your child's attention span, and

▶ your child's tolerance for frustration.

We recommend that you start with three words at a time and increase this number gradually as time permits (and your child's interest allows). Build up to a maximum of 15-20 minutes of study per day for primary students, 30 minutes per day for older students.

Most of us have forgotten phenomenal amounts of information we learned as children. Information not used is quickly forgotten. That's why it's important to review anything you teach your child. Different children will, of course, require different amounts of review. Here are some guidelines:

▶ For children of above-average ability, it may take 15-20 exposures to a new word before it becomes a part of their long-term vocabulary.

▶ For children of average or below-average ability, this may take 35-65 meaningful exposures.

Your teacher may supply you with a list of words for your child to learn. This list may be derived from your child's basal reader (reading book), or it may be a list recommended by your school system. If you aren't provided with such a list, you may want to use one of the sample lists found on pages 143 - 148. (Start with the one appropriate to your child's grade level, and move on from there.) These are widely used lists of words which occur frequently in children's books. Many of these words are not phonetically regular and are best learned by sight.

Making it fun

Homework shouldn't be boring for you or your child. Following are some suggestions for imaginative and enjoyable ways to help your child master new words. Try the ones that interest you, and use them as a starting point for coming up with your own.

▶ **Flashcards** (for learning words by sight)

For each new word:

1. Pronounce the word for your child while showing the flashcard.

2. Help your child use the word in a sentence; make sure that he or she understands it.

Variations:

1. Let your child make his or her own flashcard with crayons or markers.

2. Mix your child's flashcard with cards of other "known" words and have your child read each one. At first, words can be piled on the "correct" side if your child is able to puzzle them out. Later, this task can be made more difficult, with the word being considered "correct" only if it is recognized instantly.

As your child progresses:

1. Keep a file of words your child has learned and review them periodically.

2. Use flashcards to progress from words to phrases. (Learning to read phrases helps to move your child past simple word-by-word reading.) You can integrate these phrases into sentences and reading selections.

3. Have your child construct stories using the words he or she has learned. Reward achievement by typing your child's stories and putting them in attractive covers.

If your child needs more help remembering specific words:

1. Put a small piece of screen under the flashcard. Have your child write over the word several times, saying the word aloud each time. This reinforces verbal and aural learning with *tactile* learning.

2. Have your child draw a picture or write a sentence on the back of the flashcard.

3. Put a checkmark on the back of the flashcard every time your child says the word correctly. After 10 correct responses, remove the card from the pile and place it in a separate "word bank." Use words from the "word bank" for games or for occasional review.

▶ **Games** (for enhancing drill-and-practice)

Homemade games:

1. Make Bingo, Tic-Tac-Toe, Dominoes, or board games targeting specific words. (These can be fun family projects.) For suggestions, see pages 120 - 128.

2. Make a double set of flashcards and play Concentration (see pages 122 - 123), a game in which it's easy to add new words or replace learned words. Words read correctly can be fed into a piggy bank.

3. Invent riddles. Example: "I am thinking of a word that starts like *pet* and rhymes with *man*."

4. Adapt almost any card game for instructional purposes. Instead of matching numbers or suits, children can match words that rhyme *(hat, that)*, words that have the same vowel sound *(bake, aim)*, or words that have the same blend *(slow, sly)* or digraph *(child, chore)*, to name just a few. (A digraph is a group of two successive vowels — *oi, oy, ow, ou* — or consonants — *sh, ch, th, wh* — that form a single sound.)

HELP!

"My son brought home a list of eight words to study: **the, he, me, she, an, fan, pan,** *and* **yellow**. *He doesn't know how to begin. What can I do?"*

Six of the words can be learned by analogy with words he already knows — *be* and *man*. The other two should be learned by sight. Remind your son that he knows *be* and *man* and let him try to decode the other words with those patterns. Then make flashcards for *the* and *yellow*.

"My daughter is able to study her new words independently, but only after I have told her what they are. Should I keep telling her the words?"

Since she clearly knows how to decode some words, help her use these skills to decode those words. Then tell her the others and let her proceed independently.

How to help your child follow written directions

Children (and adults) often begin a task without bothering to read the directions first. You should encourage and expect your child to read directions — as long as they are at a level at which your child is capable of reading. If they aren't, model reading them for your child.

When directions are complex, follow these steps:

1. Read the entire set of directions aloud, slowly and carefully.

2. Underline or circle the actions(s) to be taken (the verb or verbs).

3. If the steps are not already numbered, identify and number them.

4. Help your child to follow the directions.

5. Afterward, check to make sure that the directions were followed correctly.

Children *need* to know how to read and follow directions, and this is a skill that should be taught and reinforced early. A child who can't decipher and understand directions is a child who will have difficulty completing assignments and taking tests.

How to help your child read stories

Both oral reading and silent reading are important for children of any age. Schools tend to emphasize oral reading (reading aloud) at the younger grades; this helps young children concentrate and helps teachers diagnose reading difficulties. Silent reading (reading to oneself) is faster and allows children to skim, to reread, or to adjust their speed as necessary. Because of these factors, and because adults do far more silent reading than oral reading, the emphasis shifts as the child grows older.

Young children may mumble to themselves as they read "silently." As long as they need this crutch, they should not be forced to stop using it. Even adults revert back to it when they are tired, or when they are reading something that requires a lot of concentration. If it becomes a bad habit for your child, his or her teacher can work on gradually reducing it (and you can help at home).

It is important for your child to understand what he or she is reading. Stopping too often to decode unknown words can result in the story's meaning being lost. To minimize this problem, try the following strategies:

▶ Allow your child to read through a story silently before reading it aloud. (This is particularly important for children who are self-conscious about oral reading.)

▶ Read a story aloud to your child before asking him or her to read it. (Don't be surprised if your child wants to hear the story over and over again.) This will free him or her from having to decode unknown words, will clarify the story structure, and will *make reading more enjoyable* — a very important benefit.

Granted, this strategy may result in more memorizing than reading, but it definitely has a place. As one child told us, "Reading can sure be fun when you know how!"

▶ Let your child read a favorite story into a tape recorder (preferably when there is no one around to listen). Or make a videotape of your child reading aloud. (Either an audiotape or a videotape makes an excellent keepsake for you or a grandparent.)

▶ Have your child take turns reading parts of a story with someone else — another family member, a friend, a neighbor, a sitter, even a teddy bear.

▶ Make rhyming books a regular part of your reading sessions. Turn rhymes into games by reading the beginning of each line and letting your child guess the last word.

▶ Read story beginnings aloud to your child to "hook" his or her interest, then let your child finish the story independently.

▶ Add variety to reading sessions by taking turns: you read one line, your child reads the next line, and so on through a story.

▶ If a story includes dialogue, assume the role(s) of one or more characters yourself and have your child take on another. Read "in character," using different voices, accents, and inflections.

Working with the basal reader

Almost every school uses "basal readers" — reading books with stories designed to meet specific guidelines for grade and reading level, content, and complexity. When your child brings his or her basal reader home, spend some time looking through it.

▶ DON'T, repeat DON'T encourage your child to read ahead of his or her class or group without prior approval from the teacher.

The teacher may plan to use questioning techniques which would be ineffective if the child has moved too far forward (for example, "Read____ to find out ____").

If you want to provide extra reading practice for your child — which we highly recommend — then do it with children's literature. This will in any case be superior to the basal reader. As its name indicates, the *basal* is a *base* — a starting point — and has limited vocabulary, limited sentence length and difficulty, limited story length, and limited selection, constraints not found in literature.

There are many wonderful children's books available in your school or local library. If you need help choosing, ask the librarian, who will be glad to make recommendations and point you toward children's favorites.

The following suggestions are useful for helping your child to read any story, basal or literature.

▶ *Before* **reading the story:**

1. Scan through the story to find words which may be difficult for your child to read or understand. Go over these words with your child in advance, and make flashcards if you think these are indicated.

2. Scan through the story to detect the general theme or topic. Discuss it with your child. Have your child relate it to a personal experience, if possible, or tell you what he or she already knows about it. *Then* read the story together, or have your child read it aloud to you.

3. Determine the setting of the story. If it is a real place (as opposed to a fantasy or fiction setting), and if your child is unfamiliar with it, help him or her locate it on a map or globe.

▶ *While* **reading the story:**

1. Begin by letting your child read a page or more silently.

2. Ask your child to read aloud parts of what was read silently.

3. Keep interruptions to a minimum. Supply unknown words and save phonics lessons for later so your child will not lose track of the story line or meaning. If your child misreads several words, correct *only* those which affect the meaning of the story. (For example, it's more important to correct *can't* read as *can* than *the* read as *a*.) Make less critical corrections at a time when your child misreads only a few words and comprehends well.

4. Take turns asking questions and talking about the story. Allow your child 3-5 seconds to answer questions before offering help. Questions should be varied and should cover these comprehension skills (but not all on the same day):

   • relating the story to prior knowledge ("Has anything like this ever happened to you?")

   • main ideas

   • facts from the story (who? what? when? where?)

   • recognizing a logical sequence

   • inferences (why?)

- predicting outcome ("What do you think will happen next?")

- critical thinking ("What would have happened if____? Do you agree or disagree with the author and why or why not?")

Give your child plenty of chances to initiate questions and come up with answers. This practice is vital if your child is to become an "executive reader" — one who monitors his or her own comprehension.

5. Repeat these steps at various points within the story. If, however, your child wants to get on with the story and becomes irritated with the questions, save them for the end of the selection.

HELP!

"My daughter sounds out almost every word on the page and has no idea what she is reading. What can I do?"

Your daughter may have been taught to read with an excessive dose of phonics. She needs to learn that this approach doesn't always work. Follow the steps described above in "Working with the basal reader," emphasizing the importance of reading for meaning. You may also want to let your daughter tape-record her reading. By reading and rereading passages into the tape recorder and by listening to her tapes, she may develop greater fluency.

"My son reverses letters when he reads. I'm afraid he might be dyslexic."

Just as Mommy is Mommy whether viewed from the front or the back, young children see "b" as "b" even when it's facing the other way. If such reversals persist into the third grade, talk to the teacher. Rather than immediately suspecting the presence of dyslexia — a nebulous term used differently by different professionals — try some of the solutions presented on pages 56 - 57.

"My daughter knows what most of the words in her reader say, but she does not comprehend well."

This problem could be due to one or more of the following:

▶ Your daughter's background of vocabulary and general information may not be adequate for comprehension of the material.

▶ She may be paying so much attention to saying the words "right" that she has no energy left for comprehension.

▶ She may not understand that the purpose of reading is comprehension, not word-calling.

▶ She may not know how to alter her reading speed according to her purpose for reading, and according to the demands of the material.

In any case, follow the steps described above in "Working with the basal reader."

In addition, you may want to encourage your daughter to visualize what is happening in the story. Because today's children watch so much TV, they do not form the habit of making mental pictures on their own. Try one or both of these approaches:

▶ Have your daughter draw pictures to illustrate the events in the story. Eventually she will be able to describe her mental pictures to you.

▶ Take every opportunity to work on oral comprehension. After watching a TV program together, for example, ask the questions outlined in step 4 on pages 42 - 43.

"My son comprehends stories well, even though he misreads many of the words."

Again, there may be more than one reason for this problem:

▶ Your son may be in the habit of paying little attention to what is actually written on the page.

▶ He may be having difficulty with the material and compensating by using words he does know to get a general idea of what the story is saying.

In any case, follow the steps described above in "Working with the basal reader."

"My son is in the fifth grade. He reads stories at home to prepare for reading tests, but he fails every time."

A casual reading of a story may not be sufficient preparation for a reading test in the middle grades. Meet with your son's teacher to inquire about the test format and find out what types of errors your son is making; it may be that the reading test is based on skills learned in class rather than mastery of the story content. If the test *is* story-based, you can help your son study for future tests by using the Story Study Guides on pages 149 - 150 or 151 - 152.

"My daughter reads well, both in terms of knowing what the words say and in terms of comprehending their meaning within sentences and stories. Isn't it time for her to move on to a higher-level book?"

Talk to the teacher about the possibility of advancing your daughter to the next level reader. Be aware, though, that children often perform much better at home, with one-to-one-attention, than they do in a classroom setting.

If your daughter is currently at grade level, the school may want to keep her there. Some reasons for this may include:

▶ concern over her possible lack of life experiences in dealing with above-grade materials,

▶ the desire to foster horizontal rather than vertical growth, or

▶ logistical problems: for example, the next level reading group may already be full, or it may meet at a time when your daughter has math group.

As a parent, you can probably force the issue. As a caring parent, you may want to consider whether it's worth it to do so. You always have the option of supplementing your daughter's reading at home with children's literature. Recall that this provides more richness — and more challenges — than any basal reader, even one at a higher level.

If your daughter's schoolwork starts to suffer because she's bored with her reading group, this becomes a different matter. Go back to the teacher and discuss it again, emphasizing the need for proper placement for your child.

"My son's teacher told me that he is having trouble with phonics. A friend of mine who's an elementary school teacher gave me some materials to use at home. My son did just fine on these, but the teacher still claims there is no improvement."

Different basal series teach and test reading skills in different ways. The materials supplied by your friend may address phonics or other skills in ways that your son's basal reader doesn't. Show the materials to his teacher, ask to see your son's in-class work on the same skill, and ask your son's teacher to furnish you with more supplementary materials to use at home.

Choosing other books to read at home

As you search for children's literature to share with your child, let him or her participate actively in this process. Get your child a library card (if you haven't already). Allow your child to select at least some of the books you'll be bringing home.

Naturally, you'll want to make sure that these are books your child can actually read — in other words, books that aren't too difficult or too advanced.

A good test of suitability is to have your child read the first page silently, raising a finger each time he or she comes across an unknown word. If there are more than five unknown words on the first page, try to find another, simpler book on a similar topic.

You may be surprised to discover that your child can handle material which would otherwise be out of his or her reach — *if* the material is something of keen interest to your child, or *if* the topic is one he or she already knows a lot about. The more you converse with your child, the more topics he or she will be familiar with. The moral of this story is: You can help your child's reading immeasurably by talking to him or her often and at length. As a bonus, you'll also be helping to develop your child's vocabulary and fund of general information.

How to raise your child's reading level

Here are three ways *not* to raise your child's reading level:

1. Make reading a chore that must be done for a certain amount of time every day, no matter what.

2. Tie your opinion of your child to his or her reading ability — and communicate that through your attitudes and behaviors.

3. Constantly push your child to read at a higher level.

And here is one sure way to raise your child's reading level — even if that isn't your primary goal:

1. Make reading fun.

If your child grows up loving to read, and that love of reading is at least partly due to your efforts, then you've given your child a gift that will last a lifetime.

How can you accomplish this? By keeping in mind at all times this crucial fact: Reading readiness occurs at different ages, just like the readiness to walk or talk. Typically, boys are ready later than girls, although this is not always the case. Pushing a child who is not ready can cause irreparable damage by leading to negative attitudes toward reading and a negative self-image.

In some European countries, children are taught to read at age seven. By then, most are ready, and they experience far less difficulty than many American children. This late start in no way impedes their long-term reading achievement.

Of course, this is not to say that children who are ready to read at an earlier age should be prevented from doing so. Some children can sight read words by age three; some can read and comprehend entire books by the time they start kindergarten. If your child is a "born reader," you probably already know this, and you've probably been feeding that eager young mind since you first became aware of its existence.

There is no "magical" point at which every child is ready to read, but there are several factors which indicate readiness:

▶ the ability to listen,

▶ the ability to sit still,

▶ an interest in books and in what words say,

▶ good vocabulary and language development,

▶ knowledge of the alphabet, and

▶ the ability to discriminate between different letters and sounds.

Good "first books" include picture books, rhymes, and predictable books, all of which children enjoy. (Examples: "Old MacDonald Had a Farm" and some of the simpler Bill Martin and Dr. Seuss books.) When in doubt about where to start, ask a children's librarian.

If your child has progressed beyond the beginning reader's stage, your best next step is to ease further progress. Frequent trips to the library, frequent reading-aloud sessions, and frequent parent-child conversations on a variety of topics can only heighten an interest in books that is already rooted and growing strong. The more your child reads, the better your child will read, and you will have helped to raise his or her reading level simply by doing the same things you've been doing all along.

Carole L. Riggs, while chairperson of the International Reading Association Parents and Reading Committee, compiled a list of "ABC's" for caring parents. You should find these helpful today and into the future.

THE ABC'S OF HELPING YOUR CHILD

A **Accept** your child, unconditionally.

B **Believe** in your child. Trust in his or her ability.

C **Communicate** with your child. Share ideas.

D **Discuss** things with your child.

E **Enjoy** your child. When parents enjoy their children, children enjoy their parents.

F **Find** things of interest to do together.

G **Give** your child responsibility which can be handled. This can lead to a feeling of accomplishment.

H **Help** your child with words of encouragement.

I **Impress** upon your child the vision of what is all around. Talk about the things you see, hear, taste, feel and smell.

J **Join** your child in fun activities.

K **Keep** from over-identifying with your child. Don't try to live your life again through your child.

L **Listen** to your child. He or she needs someone to share thoughts and ideas.

M **Model** behavior you want to see in your child.

N **Name** things for your child. Labels are important.

O **Observe** the way your child goes about tasks. Provide help when needed.

P **Pace** your child. Help your child to do one thing at a time and do it well.

Q **Question** your child using question words such as who, what, where and when. Ask about stories or everyday things that happen.

R **Read** to your child every day.

S **Spend** time with your child.

T **Take** your child to the library on a regular basis.

U **Understand** that learning isn't always easy. Sometimes we all fail. We can learn from our mistakes.

V **Value** your child's school and teachers. Your attitude will often be mirrored in your child.

W **Write** with your child. Encourage the youngster to write; even scribbles are important.

X **X** is often an unknown quantity. What else would you like to add to this list?

Y **You** are your child's most important teacher.

Z **Zip** it all up with love. Love gives zest to life.

Reprinted with permission of Dr. Carole L. Riggs and the International Reading Association.

We'd like to add a few "X-tras" of our own to the Reading Association's list:

▶ Remember that reading *in itself* is not fun. Reading is fun only if you are interested in what you are reading.

▶ Set aside a time and a place for reading. Allowing children to read past bedtime is one strategy that works well.

▶ Don't be limited to books. Reading material is all around us: on cereal boxes, advertisements, signs, recipes, even the backs of buses.

▶ Provide your child with a book club membership or magazine subscription of his or her own. For suggestions, see the list on page 50.

And, finally,

▶ Be a reader yourself. If your child never sees you read, he or she may learn that reading is something that is only done in school. If a boy never has a male role model of a reader, he may conclude that reading is only done by women. When your child asks you what you would like for a birthday or holiday gift, ask for a book — preferably one written by him or her.

RECOMMENDED MAGAZINES AND
A BOOK CLUB FOR CHILDREN

Art & Man, Scholastic, Inc., 730 Broadway, New York, NY 10003 (for ages 9 and up)

Boys' Life, Boy Scouts of America, 1325 Walnut Hill Lane, Irving, TX 75038-3096 (for ages 8 and up)

Cricket, Open Court Publishing Co., Box 300, Peru, IL 61354 (for ages 6 and up)

Let's Find Out, Scholastic, Inc., 730 Broadway, New York, NY 10003 (for ages 3-5)

National Geographic World, National Geographic Society, 17th and M Streets N.W., Washington, DC 20036 (for ages 9-13)

Owl, Owl & Chickadee, PO Box 11314, Des Moines, IA 50340 (for ages 8-12)

Ranger Rick, National Wildlife Federation, 1412 16th St. N.W., Washington, DC 20036

Troll Children's Book Club, 320 Route 17, Mahwah, NJ 07430

4

How To Help Your Child With Spelling and Writing

"You write with ease to show your breeding,
But easy writing's curst hard reading."
— Richard Brinsley Sheridan

How to help your child with spelling

Weekly spelling tests are a time-honored tradition in American education. However, spelling programs differ from school to school and from class to class. As you prepare to help your child with spelling, start by finding out how the program in his or her class is organized and run. Early in the school year, take these questions to a meeting with the teacher:

▶ **About the organization of the program**:

  • Is the whole class in the same spelling group?

- Is the program self-paced? (Can each child move through spelling lessons at his or her own rate?)

▶ **About your child's placement**:

- Is my child placed on, above, or below grade level in spelling?

- Is there any way for my child to move to a higher spelling group if the work proves too easy?

- Is there any way for my child to move to a lower spelling group if the work proves too difficult?

▶ **About the program schedule**:

- When are spelling words assigned?

- When is spelling homework due?

- When are spelling tests given?

▶ **About the format of the spelling test**:

- Does the test consist of words only? Or...

- Are dictated sentences included in the test?

- Does the test include other exercises, such as phonics tasks or proofreading?

▶ **About progress reports**:

- How are weekly spelling test results reported to parents?

- Are report card grades in spelling based on weekly spelling tests alone, or are they also based on spelling assignments and/or spelling on other assignments such as compositions?

These questions don't have "right" or "wrong" answers. They are designed simply to help you gather information. If there's something you don't agree with or would like to see changed, discuss it with the teacher.

How to help your child study spelling words

Each child learns differently, and this includes spelling words. The "ideal" number of study sessions, the length of study sessions, and the best method for studying will not be the same for every child. Experiment with your son or daughter to determine which approach works best — and be patient; it may take a while. Here are some suggestions for getting started.

▶ **Set up a study schedule**.

- On the day spelling words are assigned, test your child on the words for that week. Determine which are known and which need to be studied.

- Budget study time for the rest of the week. Set aside time to practice new words, and time to review previously mastered words.

- Limit spelling study sessions to 15-20 minutes each. Several shorter daily sessions are more productive than a night-before-the-test marathon cram session. Brief practices can be squeezed into spare moments: while driving to scouts, while waiting in the doctor's office, and so on.

- Plan a review of all words the night before the test.

▶ **Determine the way (or ways) your child learns best. Mix-and-match these teaching methods**:

- Have your child write each word 5, 10, or 15 times. (This works best if your child writes *all* the words one time, then *all* the words a second time, and so on.)

- Have your child type words on a typewriter or computer keyboard.

- Write each word in large letters for your child. Then have him or her trace each one with a finger and pronounce it while tracing. Repeat until your child can write the word from memory.

- Dictate each word to your child and have him or her write it down. Then have your child correct the paper or slate. This encourages closer attention to mistakes.

- Say the words into a tape recorder. Leave enough "lag time" after each so your child can write the word. This will permit repeated practices — as many as necessary, and as many as the child wants — with minimal parental involvement.

"My son and I work on spelling words for at least an hour every Thursday night for the test on Friday. Yet he still fails his spelling tests. Our study sessions are tiring, tension-producing, and obviously nonproductive."

The following sample schedule may help improve your son's productivity and make the study experience more enjoyable for both of you. Remember to keep study sessions short (no more than 15-20 minutes).

SAMPLE SPELLING STUDY SCHEDULE

MONDAY

1. Pretest on the whole list
2. Teach 1/3 of the words missed on the pretest
3. Test on all words learned so far

TUESDAY

1. Test on all words learned to date
2. Teach the second 1/3 of words missed on Monday's pretest
3. Test on all words learned so far

WEDNESDAY

1. Test on all words learned to date
2. Teach the third 1/3 of words missed on Monday's pretest
3. Test on all words learned so far

THURSDAY

1. Test on all words learned to date
2. Practice the most difficult words
3. Test again

FRIDAY

1. Send your child off to school with these words: "We practiced for your spelling test all week. We know you're prepared. Do the best you can today, and however you do will be fine with me."

Perhaps this scene has been played out in your home: one day your third-grader, who is intelligent, studious and gets good grades, comes up against an unfamiliar kind of test. The teacher says it's important and passes out test booklets, answer sheets and special pencils. Instead of being friendly and helpful, the teacher remains cool, won't answer questions and keeps warning the class about the time limit. Panicky and upset, your son finishes the test and comes home in tears, convinced he has done poorly. Sure enough, when his score is computed, it is well below what his previous record might have predicted.

This is no insignificant setback. As schools rely more and more

Here are ways for parents to help their children with those all-important standardized tests

How to Improve Your Child's Test Scores

By Edwin Kiester, Jr., and Sally Valente Kiester

piece of paper with the words: "Don't Forget—Shake 'n' Ache." Curiosity got the better of me and so I asked, "What do you mean by 'shake and ache'?"

"It's a reminder to go to my aerobics class," she replied.

—HENRY BOTWINICK (Brooklyn, N.Y.)

WE FOUND a charming bed-and-breakfast place nestled in the White Mountains of New Hampshire. Though enchanted, I nonetheless had some questions about the accommodations. "Does the room have its own bath?" I asked.

The proprietor's answer was terse and to the point: "If no one else comes, it does."

—JOSEPH J. SOLTYS (Storrs, Conn.)

SATURDAY had always been "cleaning day" in the old homestead, and my mother still adhered to the ritual after all her children had left the nest. When I stopped by to visit her one Saturday, I was surprised to find her relaxing in a favorite chair. "Aren't you feeling well?" I asked.

"I feel fine."

"But you're not cleaning."

"After all these years I've finally figured out how to get it done in half the time," Mom told me. "I simply take off my glasses."

—PAT MILLIS (New Castle, Ind.)

MY HUSBAND, who is in his 70s, returned from playing golf one afternoon and announced that he and his partner had joined up with two attractive young women. "They turned out to be real good golfers too," he added.

"Did you learn anything from them?" I asked.

"I learned that it's impossible to hold my stomach in for two hours!"

—KAY GAMMONS (Cape Elizabeth, Maine)

WE WERE SELLING our house and received an unexpected call that prospective buyers were on the way. My husband and I began a mad scramble to tidy up before they arrived. He headed to the guest room where unfolded laundry was piled on the bed, while I got rid of a sinkful of dirty dishes. Finished, I went into the guest room.

There was a massive bulge under the bedspread. "Shhh," my husband whispered, winking at me. "Aunt Bertha is sleeping."

—DEBBY GLASSCOCK (Loveland, Colo.)

SOON AFTER we moved from a large city to a rural town, the hula-hoop craze had a revival. My four-year-old daughter wanted one, and I went to the only toy store in the area. They were out of stock.

At the hardware store, I was telling a sympathetic salesman how disappointed my daughter had been. "We don't sell hula hoops but . . . wait a minute," he said, and disappeared. When he returned, he was carrying plastic tubing. Joining the ends with a coupling, he presented me with a handmade "hoop."

"How much do I owe you?" I asked gratefully.

His answer brought home to me the warmth of small-town living. "Nothing," he said gruffly. "I told you we don't sell hula hoops."

—SANDY HARDIN (Brownsville, Tenn.)

Contributors of stories published in this department receive $400. For further information, see page 2.

83

"Every Monday my daughter's teacher writes the week's spelling words on the board. Every Monday afternoon my daughter comes home with a list of misspelled words to study. We never know what to study because she doesn't have a spelling book. I have read notes written by the teacher, so I can safely assume that the teacher is writing the words on the board correctly."

Meet with the teacher to determine the root of your daughter's problem. She may have difficulty copying from the board, and she may need her vision checked. Or she may be perfectly capable of copying the words but is not taking the time to do so.

"Every week I give my son his spelling words and he spells them out loud to me, but then he fails his weekly spelling test. How can he know the words so well and not manage to pass the tests?"

Practicing spelling words orally is only one way to learn them, and it may not be the best way for your son. Try some of the other strategies outlined on page 53. Make sure that your son practices *writing* the words, not just saying them.

"My daughter gets 100% on every spelling test. Do I really need to help her study each week?"

It may be sufficient to pretest her on the day spelling words are assigned and let her work independently from there. If she continues to ace the test, however, you may want to schedule a conference with the teacher to find out why. Possible reasons include:

▶ The spelling list words may not be challenging enough for your daughter. She may need to be moved to a higher spelling group, or be given a list of supplemental challenge words to work on.

▶ The words may be of an appropriate level of difficulty, but the teacher may provide enough in-class drill that practice at home is not necessary.

Making it fun

Spelling is easily taught through the use of games — commercial games like *Scrabble* and *Speak 'n' Spell*, and homemade games like Hangman. See chapter 8 for suggestions.

How to help your child with handwriting

Helping your child with handwriting takes patience, patience, and more patience. Many children simply don't like the process of writing by hand. (Many adults don't, either. Why else are typewriters and word processors so popular?) We know one young boy who will gladly spend hours making elaborate drawings of buildings, cars, airplanes, and other complicated subjects, yet the moment he's asked to write a sentence he wails, "I CAN'T! It's TOO HARD!"

Nevertheless, all children *must* master these skills to some degree. With firm and caring assistance, even the most reluctant writer will eventually come around!

When to worry about letter and word reversals

Among reading professionals, a great deal of controversy exists around the topic of letter and word reversals. For example, many experts maintain that reversals are not the *cause* of learning problems but a *symptom*. They disagree among themselves about the best way to approach this issue and which remedial tactics are most effective. Naturally, this controversy has led to widespread confusion among parents.

All children who make reversals do not "have dyslexia," any more than all thin children have anorexia nervosa. Before concluding that your child has learning problems, consider the following:

▶ Reversals are quite common among children in the primary grades. They usually begin to subside by age 8 or 9.

▶ Reversals of the letters *b* and *d* can sometimes be eliminated if the child is taught this simple trick: Have the child make two fists with thumbs stuck up to form a "bed." The *b* in the word *bed* is its head (left hand); the *d* is its foot (right hand). (Since most children write on their hands anyway, go ahead and give your child permission to do it this time. The lesson will be even more unforgettable.)

▶ If the problem persists, or if the reversals are coupled with other obvious learning problems, consider having your child professionally evaluated. Ask the teacher about the school's procedures or seek outside testing.

Improving your child's printing

Many children have difficulty learning to print. If your child does, this may be due to one or more reasons:

▶ insufficient in-class practice time,

▶ lack of interest in writing,

▶ the failure to realize that legible writing is an important means of communication, and/or

▶ slow development of fine motor coordination.

There are many ways to help your child improve his or her printing skills. Experiment with the following techniques, or ask the teacher for additional suggestions. See pages 153 - 157 for charts and practice paper you can use for practice sessions.

Before having your child practice either the traditional Zaner-Bloser or the newer D'Nealian style of printing, check with the teacher to find out which is being taught in school. Also make sure that your sequence or pacing of instruction does not conflict with the teacher's plan for the year.

▶ Allow 10-15 minutes per night, 4 nights per week for printing practice.

▶ Teach 4 letters per week for 13 weeks. Start with the lower-case letters, then move on to the capital letters.

Once your child has learned a few letters, use the following routine to ready him or her for forming words:

1. During each week's first practice session, have your child practice the first two letters of the week on manuscript practice paper. See page 157 for a sample suitable for photocopying.

2. During each week's second practice session, have your child practice the letters in real words on manuscript practice paper. Assign words that position the new letter at the *beginning*, the *middle*, and the *end*. Examples: see, must, pets.

3. Repeat steps 1 and 2 for the remaining two letters and the next two practice sessions.

4. During each week's final practice session, have your child review all letters learned to date. For this practice, your child should use regular writing paper rather than manuscript practice paper.

Keep practice sessions brief and fun. Permit the use of colored pencils, crayons, and various other writing instruments to further motivate your child.

Following each practice session, have your child examine his or her writing and identify ways it can be improved. The "3S" method is one way to approach this. Your child asks himself or herself these questions about each letter:

▶ Is the letter the right SIZE?

▶ Is the letter the right SHAPE?

▶ Did I leave enough SPACE between letters and words?

Encourage your child to write by posting practice pages on the refrigerator or sending them to grandparents or other admiring adults.

Improving your child's cursive

Many children have difficulty making the transition from printing (manuscript) writing to cursive (script) writing. If your child does, this may be due to one or more reasons:

▶ Insufficient class time may be devoted to teaching and practicing cursive.

▶ Your child may have problems writing individual letters.

▶ Your child may be able to write the letters correctly but have problems connecting them.

▶ Comments from the teacher may be so general ("Your handwriting is messy") that they give no real direction for improvement.

▶ Your child may simply not like to write, and as a result may be hasty and careless with letter and word formation.

It is our experience that with regular, systematic, intensive practice in cursive writing, most intermediate students can substantially improve their formation and connection of cursive letters. And once they learn to write correctly, their speed and attitude improve.

We believe that children should be allowed to write in whichever way is most comfortable for them — printing *or* cursive — after they have perfected both modes. We also believe that children should be taught to use the typewriter if all else fails. We offer the following suggestions for helping your child master cursive. See pages 159 - 163 for charts and practice paper you can use for practice sessions.

We have found that practice paper is especially effective in motivating children to develop a uniform size and slant for their cursive letters. Colored magic markers (the thin-point, felt-tipped variety) make it fun and easy because they literally glide across the page.

One more tip before you begin: Cursive practice is more than an intellectual learning process; it's also a *physical* learning process. The hand, wrist, arm, elbow, and shoulder must be taught specific patterns of movement. The more your child practices, the more habitual these patterns will become. (In a way, learning to write cursive is a lot like learning to ride a bicycle.)

▶ Allow 10-15 minutes per night, 4 nights per week for cursive practice.

▶ Teach 4 letters per week for 13 weeks. Start with the lower-case letters, then move on to the capital letters.

1. During each week's first practice session, have your child practice the first two letters of the week on cursive practice paper. See page 163 for a sample suitable for photocopying.

2. During each week's second practice session, have your child practice the letters in real words on cursive practice paper. Assign words that position the new letter at the *beginning*, the *middle*, and the *end*. Examples: **b**ook, a**b**le, so**b**.

3. Repeat steps 1 and 2 for the remaining two letters and the next two prac-
    tice sessions.

4. During each week's final practice session, have your child review all letters
    learned to date. For this practice, your child should use regular writing
    paper rather than cursive practice paper.

Keep practice sessions brief and fun. Permit the use of colored pencils,
crayons, and various other writing instruments to further motivate your child.

Following each practice session, have your child examine his or her writing
and find ways it can be improved. The "4S" method is one way to approach
this. Your child asks himself or herself these questions about each letter:

▶   Is the letter the right SIZE?

▶   Is the letter the right SHAPE?

▶   Are all the letters SLANTED in the same direction and at the same
    angle?

▶   Did I leave enough SPACE between letters and words?

Supplement practice sessions with opportunities for "real" writing. Invite
your child to help you prepare party invitations, shopping lists, and thank-you
notes. Encourage him or her to write letters to grandparents or friends.

HELP!

*"My daughter's handwriting is AWFUL! When she was in the primary grades,
her papers were just fine. But now that she is in third grade and has to use cursive, her teacher is constantly writing negative comments on her papers."*

Talk with the teacher to discover the source of your daughter's problem.
Cursive is usually introduced in the third grade, so the teacher is right on
schedule. Your daughter may simply need more practice than other children in
her class. Make regular practice sessions a part of her daily homework schedule.

*"My son knows how to make all of his cursive letters, yet his papers are still a
mess. He refuses to slow down and write neatly."*

Your son needs to understand that legible writing is a form of good man-
ners. When our writing is messy, we're implying that we don't care whether

someone else can read it or not. Also, many people judge others by their written work. Tidy, readable writing makes a good first impression that lasts.

Let your son use a stopwatch or a kitchen timer during his practice sessions. Encourage him to work quickly, but neatly. Emphasize that it is possible to write rapidly in cursive while maintaining legibility.

"My son's cursive is beautiful. The teacher admits that he can write better than she does! Is it really necessary for him to participate in cursive lessons and practices at school?"

Probably not, but talk to the teacher *before* expressing this opinion to your son. If he has genuine talent and interest in this area, you may want to explore the possibility of signing him up for calligraphy lessons. Meanwhile, encourage him to help you with addressing greeting cards, invitations, and so on — opportunities to show off his skill.

How to raise your child's grades in English

The English curriculum (also known as "language" or "language arts") may include language mechanics, handwriting, spelling, and composition. It varies greatly from school to school and from text to text. As a result, there are no blanket cure-alls for children who experience difficulty in this area.

You may find significant differences between the English curriculum today and the curriculum you grew up with. Most current textbooks tend to have fewer of those grammar exercises we all dreaded. Instead, grammar is now taught more through composition, and students see why they are learning grammar as they apply what has been taught.

If your child is earning low grades in English, schedule a conference with the teacher. Let the teacher know that you want to help your child and ask for recommendations. Inquire about state minimum requirements and skills that must be mastered for yearly tests (often called "benchmarks").

"How to improve your child's composition" on pages 63 - 67 includes many suggestions you should find helpful as you work with your child.

HELP!

"My son has not passed a single English test this year. He never seems to know when tests are scheduled, and he never brings his book home to study. How can I possibly help him?"

Most English books do not conform to the same neat "one-lesson-a-week, test-every-Friday" format as spelling texts. Some lessons may last for less than a week; others may take up two weeks or more of class time. Find out from your son's teacher how lessons are set up in the text and when tests are scheduled. Ask for extra practice activities and materials your son can complete at home prior to the tests.

"My daughter usually performs well in language arts, but she has real trouble with punctuation. She failed the last three tests and will probably get a C for this grading period. Should I just forget about this problem and assume that her grade will improve as soon as the class moves on to a new unit?"

Even though your daughter's overall grade may be respectable, it's never a good idea to "skip over" an entire set of skills. Knowing how to punctuate is essential, and if she doesn't learn it now, she will have to learn it later. (Punctuation skills are often included on minimum skills tests.) Ask the teacher for extra practice activities and materials your daughter can complete at home. And find out which punctuation skills are included on minimum skills tests your daughter will take this year; at the very least, she should master these.

"My son is a whiz in English. His grades have been top-notch all year. But he never brings his book home, so I don't know what he's studying. How can I be sure that he's learning all the skills he needs to score well on our state's basic skills test?"

Talk to his teacher or the academic advisor at your school. Find out how the classroom curriculum correlates with your state's basic skills test. Most schools are very conscious of state requirements and have planned their lessons to promote success on basic skills tests. A conference should provide you with the information you need to feel comfortable about this.

How to improve your child's composition

Perhaps the most important qualification you can bring to this task is...patience. Often children (and adults) are anxious to complete a written task and are satisfied with one draft. If children can learn the value of the prewriting-writing-revising process at an early age, their writing will be greatly improved for now and the future.

We recommend these steps:

1. **Brainstorm.**

Before actually beginning a composition, your child should be encouraged to *brainstorm* — to generate and list ideas. You can participate, too, as long as you play equal roles. In other words, a brainstorming session is no time to exercise parental authority or to insist that your ideas are the "right" ones.

Brainstorming as a technique is used in classrooms, companies, and businesses across the country to promote creative thinking and problem-solving. Fun for all, it has only three simple rules:

- Everyone tries to generate as many ideas as possible — from serious to outrageous and everything in between.

- Any idea is considered acceptable during the brainstorming session. (Save the weeding out for later.)

- Nobody is allowed to criticize anybody else's ideas.

The more ideas are generated, the more successful the session will be. If your child's writing skills are not at the point where he or she can write quickly, then you should assume responsibility for listing the ideas as they're spoken.

What kinds of ideas can help with a composition assignment? For example, if your child's assignment is to "describe your favorite person," he or she can brainstorm characteristics of the person chosen and reasons why that person is worth writing about.

2. **Organize.**

Once enough ideas have been generated, your child should organize them in a logical order. A formal outline may not be necessary, but some effort should be made to arrange the details in some kind of sequence.

3. **Write the first draft.**

After the general sequence has been determined, your child should write a *rough* first draft. Pay no attention at this stage to the fine points of spelling or punctuation; the purpose of the first draft is to get something (anything!) down on the page.

4. **Revise.**

Revisions not only take patience; they also require attention to detail. It's hard at first for young writers to revise their own work because they have not yet internalized grammar rules, and they may not see their own spelling mistakes.

The "A-OK" method is one way to make revising easier and more efficient. It directs the child to focus on one aspect of the composition at a time. Introduce it by modeling — taking your child through each step and showing how it's done. Eventually your child should be able to handle it independently.

A-OK has five steps: "MOK," "POK," "SOK," "WOK," and "NOK." Each step contains two or more questions for your child to ask. How much revising is necessary depends on how your child answers the questions.

A-OK

I.   **MOK ("meaning OK")**

- Does it make sense?

- Are my facts correct?

- Did I say what I really wanted to say?

II. **POK ("paragraph OK")**

- Is it indented?

- Is it made up of sentences related to ONE main idea?

- Is it connected logically with paragraphs that come before or after?

III. **SOK ("sentence OK")**

- Does it start with a capital letter?

- Does it end with the correct punctuation mark?

- Does it express a complete thought?

IV. WOK ("word OK")

- Is it spelled correctly?

- Is it capitalized correctly (if it needs to be)?

- Is it the VERY BEST word, or is there another, better word I could use in its place?

V. NOK ("neatness OK")

- Is it easy to read?

- Does it follow the form required by my teacher? (Typed? Every other line? Written on one side of the paper only? In a folder?)

Adapted with permission from "A-OK: A Reading for Revision Strategy" by Jeanne Shay Schumm in *Reading: Exploration and Discovery*, Vol. 10, No. 1, Fall, 1987.

Revising is one step of the writing process that is greatly simplified with a word processor. Children who are reluctant to revise on paper may be much more willing to do so when each revision doesn't involve a complete rewrite. With the freedom a word processor provides, and the extra work it saves, even children who don't like to write turn out better papers. For more information on word processing, see pages 7 - 9.

One final note: Whenever possible, revising should be done out loud. Errors are easier to catch when they are said and heard than when they are read silently.

HELP!

"My daughter's stories seem more like lists of words than paragraphs. There is no capitalization or punctuation. She is in the fourth grade; shouldn't her composition skills be better than this?"

Your daughter could benefit from regular writing practice. Start by giving her short but interesting things to write — postcards to friends or relatives, invitations, descriptions of her favorite TV shows, and so on. Begin working on the sentence level. Show your daughter that each sentence begins with a capital letter and ends with a punctuation mark. After she writes a sentence, have her read it out loud and revise it using the appropriate steps of the A-OK method.

As she becomes more comfortable with her writing, encourage her to move on to longer, more sophisticated sentences. Demonstrate with a basic sentence, then slowly add and edit words to embellish it. For example:

"I saw a girl."

"I saw a little girl."

"I saw a pretty little girl."

"I noticed a pretty little girl wearing red overalls."

"I noticed a pretty little girl wearing red overalls and skating backwards down the sidewalk."

Once your daughter feels confident about "SOKing" and "WOKing" sentences, she'll be ready to progress to the paragraph level and from there to more complex compositions.

"My son writes interesting compositions and stories for school, but his grades are never very good because his spelling is poor. I can't figure out why he misspells words in compositions that he has spelled correctly on spelling tests."

Chances are that your son's imagination is working faster than his pencil. He's concerned with ideas over form. Congratulate him on his creativity, and let it continue to run free — on the first draft. Then insist that he use the A-OK method to revise it *before* he hands it in for a grade. You may need to go through these steps with him several times before he can do them by himself.

Meanwhile, have him keep a list of his misspelled words. He will become aware of which words he is missing, and you can take this opportunity to help him learn to spell them correctly. Look back at pages 52 - 55, "How to help your child study spelling words," for suggestions.

If your son consistently has problems spelling while writing, you may want to consider adding a book to the reference library in his study center: *How To Spell It: A Dictionary of Commonly Misspelled Words* by Harriet Wittels and Joan Greisman (New York: Grosset & Dunlap, 1973). This book is actually a 330-page word list (without definitions) that includes both correct *and* incorrect spellings. The correct spellings are shown in red; the incorrect spellings are shown in black. A child can look up a word the way he or she *thinks* it should be spelled — and easily find the way it *should* be spelled. You may not find *How To Spell It* in your local bookstore, but you can ask them to order it for you from the publisher. Or write: Grosset & Dunlap, Inc., The Putnam Publishing Group, 200 Madison Ave., New York, NY 10016.

"My daughter always receives high grades on her compositions. She seems to have a real talent for writing. Is there something I could be doing to encourage her?"

You can introduce her to ways she might win prizes for her writing or get published. Many civic organizations sponsor writing competitions; check with the teacher, media specialist, or children's librarian. Many publications, local and national, provide space in their issues for children's writing (and some are entirely child-written). A list of publications is given on page 68.

If your daughter seems interested in submitting her work for publication, take her to the library for an afternoon of exploring those magazines the library subscribes to. To see copies of the others, write to the publishers and request samples. (You may be charged a small fee.) Help your daughter examine these thoroughly to determine what kinds of writing get published. Then let *her* decide if she wants to give it a try. Bolster her confidence when and if she receives rejection notices — and tell her to keep trying.

You can also encourage her to share her writing with family and friends. For example, she could make books of her short stories or poems and give them as gifts on special occasions.

PUBLICATIONS AND PUBLISHERS
THAT ACCEPT WORK BY YOUNG WRITERS

Child Life
1100 Waterway Boulevard
PO Box 567
Indianapolis, IN 46206

Children's Playmate
1100 Waterway Boulevard
PO Box 567
Indianapolis, IN 46206

Creative Kids
PO Box 6448
Mobile, AL 36660

Cricket
Box 300
Peru, IL 61354

SPIN-OFF
Gifted Children Monthly
PO Box 115
Sewell, NJ 08080

Highlights for Children
PO Box 269
Columbus, OH 43272-0002

Jack and Jill
PO Box 567
Indianapolis IN 46206

Know Your World EXTRA
245 Long Hill Road
Middletown, CT 06457

Language Arts
1111 Kenyon Rd.
Urbana, IL 61801

READ
245 Long Hill Road
Middletown, CT 06457

Stone Soup
PO Box 83
Santa Cruz, CA 95063

5

How To Help Your Child With Math

"A child's mind is like a bank — whatever you put in, you get back in ten years, with interest."
— Frederic Wertham

How to help your child with math facts and computation

Many parents are less comfortable helping their children with math than almost any other subject. While it's fairly easy to look up the correct spelling of a word in a dictionary, there are no "dictionaries" that list the correct answers to math problems. In other words, you have to know how to work them *yourself* before you can help your child check his or her answers. Be thankful that calculus is reserved for the later grades!

The reality is that most of us adults are lazy about using math in our daily lives. We reach for our calculators when it's time to balance our checkbooks or figure our taxes. Nevertheless, there are certain math facts and skills that our children will have to learn in school. This chapter provides guidelines you can use to help your child without suffering too much "math anxiety" of your own.

Teaching math facts

A child who knows math facts can instantly give answers to addition, subtraction, multiplication, and division number sentences in which two of the numbers are generally one-digit numbers. (For example: 3 + 6, 7 - 2, 8 x 8, 49 ÷ 9.) Before you start teaching math facts to your child, check with the teacher to find out the sequence of lessons for the year. Look through your child's math book when he or she brings it home, and preview the pages to be learned or worked on before beginning each homework session.   Don't encourage your child to work ahead in the book without getting prior approval from the teacher.

▶ Generally speaking, math facts using low numbers should be taught first. There are exceptions: for example, the multiplication tables which are easiest to teach (and learn) are the 0's, 1's, 2's, 5's, 10's, and 11's.

▶ "Skip counting" — for example, counting by 2's or 3's — can be useful when helping a child learn multiplication. One of the best tools we've found for teaching this technique is an audiotape called "Skip Count Kid and Friends: Musical Multiplication Tape." Write: James R. McGhee II, 8200 SW 130 St., Miami, FL 33156.

▶ Related math facts should be taught together. For example, "3 + 5" should be taught with "5 + 3," and "8 - 3" should be taught with "8 - 5." Practice gained by filling in addition and multiplication tables can help children discover some of these relationships. See pages 165 and 167 for sample grids you can use.

▶ Math facts should be learned in small doses. As a rule of thumb, three new facts are sufficient for one session.

▶ Math facts should be taught in different formats. Mix-and-match these methods:

  •   Present the problem orally. (Ask "What's 3 + 4?")

  •   Write the problem vertically:

$$\begin{array}{r} 3 \\ +\ 4 \\ \hline 7 \end{array}$$

- Write the problem horizontally:

  3 + 4 = 7

- Alternate between writing on paper and writing on flashcards or on a slate.

Your child should be able to recognize the same fact regardless of which way it's presented.

▶ Math facts should be reviewed often. Frequent short sessions (10 minutes or so) are usually more effective than infrequent long sessions. An excellent, inexpensive home video which can be used for multiplication fact review is "Multiplication Rock." Write: Golden Book Videos, c/o Western Publishing Co., Inc., 1220 Mound Ave., Racine, WI 53404.

We recommend that you start helping your child to *overlearn* math facts as soon as they are introduced in class. Often parents wait until after their child's teacher says that the child is experiencing difficulty. While it's never too late, it's certainly simpler and more pleasant to exercise preventive teaching.

Even after your child appears to know and understand the math facts appropriate to his or her grade level, they should still be practiced frequently. Aim to "program" them into your child's brain so thoroughly that he or she can answer problems without having to figure them out.

Helping with computation

▶ Familiarize yourself with the procedures your child is being taught in school so you do not inadvertently confuse him or her by using other procedures. For example, in long division, the teacher may want the children to fill in 0's where you were taught to leave empty spaces, like this:

$$
\begin{array}{r}
98 \\
18\,)\overline{1764} \\
\underline{1620} \\
144 \\
\underline{144} \\
000
\end{array}
$$

▶ Some teachers require children to copy problems before working them (a practice we recommend over simply filling in blanks on worksheets). Have your child check to see that problems were copied correctly.

▶ Don't let your child practice a mathematical operation incorrectly. If he or she is getting wrong answers, ask your child to explain how he or she arrived at the answers. This should help you determine the underlying cause for the difficulty. Possible causes include:

- insufficient knowledge of math facts,

- carelessness, and

- poor understanding of the computation process.

If poor understanding turns out to be the cause, ask the teacher for suggestions. (Make sure that *you* understand the process being taught at school.) Or have your child leave that page or assignment undone. Write a note to the teacher explaining what you think is the source of the problem. This will be a sign to the teacher that further instruction is necessary.

▶ Resist the urge to correct your child's computation errors. Instead, encourage your child to proofread and correct his or her own problems. Doing the reverse operation is a preferred way of proofreading. For example:

$$\begin{array}{r} 42 \\ -\ 19 \\ \hline 23 \end{array} \longleftrightarrow \begin{array}{r} 23 \\ +\ 19 \\ \hline 42 \end{array}$$

When to worry about a child who counts on his or her fingers

We all learn better with concrete aids. Think about how difficult it would be to learn to bake a cake without actually doing it. Consider how hard it would be to *tell* someone how to tie a pair of shoelaces without actually demonstrating it.

Young children in particular need concrete aids when learning math facts and computation. And if there's one thing they can always count on to be there for them, it's their own 10 fingers.

The age at which children outgrow this varies from child to child. If your child is still doing it by the third or fourth grade, talk to the teacher and find out what other aids are allowable. This is especially important if the teacher penalizes children for counting on their fingers.

Making it fun

There are many fun and interesting ways to practice math facts and computation; see chapter 8 for suggestions. You may want to purchase one or more of the commercial games that teach or reinforce these skills — *Quizmo*, for example, or *Yahtzee*. Flashcards and computer software are other options for you to explore. For a list of recommended programs, see page 116.

Whenever possible, these skills should be taught in meaningful, real-life contexts. Supervise your child as he or she makes a minor purchase at a store and keeps the change (counting it afterward to make sure it's right). Open a savings account for your child at a local bank. Let your child take his or her weekly allowance out of a pile of coins. You can probably think of dozens more ways to bring math into your daily activities with your child.

There are also several "tricks" that can take the drudgery out of math facts and computation. (They can also serve as a source of pride for your child, since other children may not know them.) For example, you might lead your child to discover that adding 9 is the same as adding 10 and taking away 1, or that subtracting 9 is the same as subtracting 10 and adding 1.

Following are more tricks for you to try with your child.

▶ **For teaching fraction reductions and division:**

- Numbers that end in a multiple of 2 are divisible by 2. (Examples: 4, 38, 576, even 1,395,405,778.)

- Numbers whose last two digits are a multiple of 4, or whose last three digits are a multiple of 8, are divisible by 4 and 8, respectively. (Example: Since 56 is divisible by 4, so is 1,356.)

- Numbers whose digits add up to multiples of 3 or 9 are divisible by 3 or 9, respectively. (For example, the digits in 378 add up to 18. Since 18 is divisible by both 3 and 9, so is 378.)

- Numbers that end in 5 or 0 are divisible by 5.

- Numbers that end in 0 are divisible by 10.

▶ **For teaching multiplication:**

- The "Nines Trick" illustrated on the following pages works for the nines tables. Model it for your child, who will probably be eager to imitate you.

Number your fingers from 1-10.

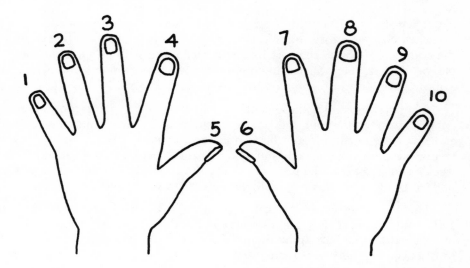

Let's say that the problem you want to demonstrate is "9 x 7." Flex the "7" finger. Everything to the *left* of that finger is the tens; everything to the *right* of that finger is the ones. There are 6 fingers to the left and 3 fingers to the right, so the product is 63.

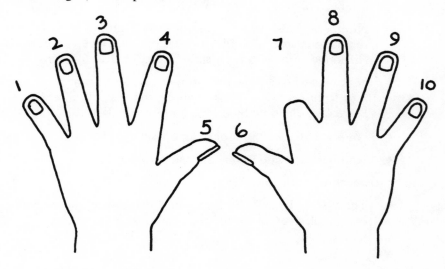

This trick can also be used for division when the divisor is 9. For example, to find

9) 63,

flex the finger that would separate 6 tens from 3 ones. That would be the "7" finger, making the quotient 7.

- The "Sluggard's Rule" works when both factors are from 6-10 inclusive. (This trick, also called "finger multiplication," was introduced by Dantzig in 1941.) It is more difficult than the "Nines Trick" and should be taught only after that trick has been mastered. Your child will need to know the multiplication tables up through "4 x 4" in order to use this trick. Again, you should model it for your child, not just describe it.

Start by numbering the fingers on each of your hands from 6-10, beginning with the thumbs.

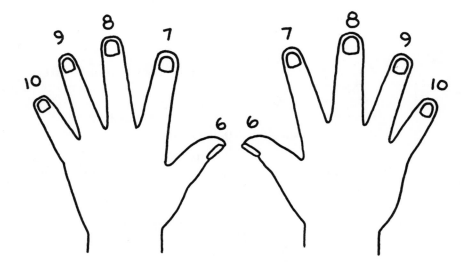

To find the product of "8 x 7," touch the "8" finger of one hand to the "7" finger of the other hand. Flex the fingers numbered higher than the two that are touching (the "9" and "10," and the "8," "9," and "10"). Add the number of the outstretched fingers (including the two that are touching) to get the tens. Multiply the number of flexed fingers on one hand by the number of flexed fingers on the other hand to get the ones.

In this example, 3 + 2 = 5 for the tens, and 2 x 3 = 6 for the ones, making the product 56.

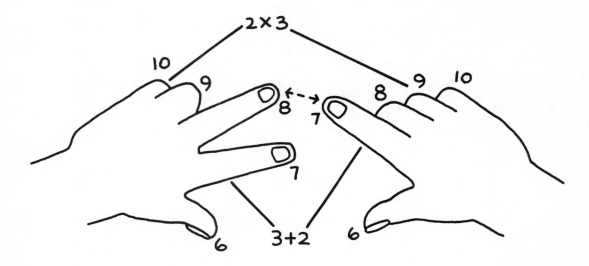

For "6 x 6" and "7 x 6," a bit of extra computation is necessary. With "6 x 6" there would be 1 finger up on each hand, making two tens (1 + 1). Then there would be 4 fingers flexed on each hand, making the ones' product 16. This product must be added to the 20 (2 tens) for the tens, making the final product 20 + 16 = 36.

This strategy may sound complicated, but never underestimate the child who is desperate to find some "magical" way of figuring out multiplication facts.

HELP!

"My daughter is a fifth grader who doesn't know her multiplication facts. She takes forever to do her homework. Should I let her use a calculator?"

Find out if her teacher has a plan for helping students master multiplication facts. If so, you can reinforce it at home. If the teacher isn't using a particular plan, have your daughter practice with flashcards. Meanwhile, you can let her use a calculator for long multiplication problems. This will enable her to concentrate on the process without being held back by her lack of knowledge. Once she understands the process, she can return to multiplying on her own and use the calculator to check her answers.

Most children would prefer to do *all* of their math homework on a calculator — not because they're lazy (although this may be the case), but also because calculators are fun to use. Some children will spend blissful hours punching numbers in and watching them appear on the display. To reinforce learning during play, you may want to provide a calculator that functions like an adding machine, printing whole problems as well as the answers.

"My son needs a lot of help with his math homework, but the terms used in his text are different from the ones I learned when I was in school. I'm discovering, for example, that 'trading,' 'borrowing,' and 'regrouping' can all mean the same thing. How can I help him without confusing him?"

If your son can't define the terms himself, you may be able to check their meanings by looking at the sample problems in his math book or checking the glossary. Some basic terms are provided here for your reference.

BASIC COMPUTATIONAL TERMS

```
  addend              factor
+ addend            x factor
---------           ---------
  sum                product

  minuend              quotient  (+ remainder)
- subtrahend       divisor ) dividend
----------
  difference
```

"My son's math homework is sloppy. Since he doesn't line his numbers up correctly, he makes mistakes with 2-digit addition and subtraction problems."

Have his vision checked by an ophthalmologist or optometrist; his problem may be visual. Or he may be working too fast and may simply need to slow down. If his problem is severe, let him use graph paper with large squares, or turn his regular writing paper around so the lines are vertical rather than horizontal. Then have him write numbers between the lines, as in the example shown below. After completing his homework, he can copy the problems on clean paper in the standard fashion.

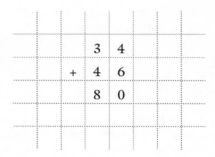

"My daughter does well in math, but she sometimes makes careless errors. What can I do?"

Your daughter should get in the habit of proofreading her work. If she can't spot errors when going over the problems, she can redo them on a separate sheet of paper.

Or she can perform the opposite operation and compare her results. For example, a division problem can be proved by multiplying the quotient times the divisor and adding any remainder to obtain the dividend.

If the problem is to divide 47 by 7 and she comes up with this answer,

$$
\begin{array}{r}
6, \text{ remainder } 5 \\
7\,)\overline{47} \\
\underline{42} \\
5
\end{array}
$$

she can check it with this computation:

6 x 7 + 5 = 47.

The point is that both redoing problems and performing opposite operations are repetitive and time-consuming. Either procedure may teach your daughter to be more careful the first time around.

How to help your child with math concepts

Like math facts, math concepts should be taught in logical sequences. Start by familiarizing yourself with your child's math text so you can understand its sequence of instruction. Check with the teacher to find out if he or she will be using the materials in a different sequence or supplementing them with others.

The more informed you are, the more you will be able to help your child.

Addition, subtraction, multiplication, division, fractions, and decimals

As noted earlier, any learning is easier with concrete aids. Start with body parts (like fingers and toes), follow with other concrete objects (like pennies and buttons), and end up with abstract numbers, and you will have made these basic concepts much more accessible to your child.

Children need to understand that addition and subtraction are opposite operations, as are multiplication and division. They also need to understand that multiplication is a fast way of adding, and that division is a fast way of subtracting. Proving answers by performing opposite operations can help bring home these concepts.

The concept of decimals is best taught with money. Using coins and bills to indicate the difference between $0.50, $5.00, and $50.00 can make light-bulbs go on over children's heads. Once children have learned decimals with money, it's easy for them to understand decimals overall.

Fractions can be more difficult to grasp. A child may quite reasonably wonder how 1/5 can be smaller than 1/4, since 5 is more than 4. Or, when 1 of 3 parts of a circle is colored in, why is this part 1/3 instead of 1/2, since 1 part is colored in and 2 parts aren't? Use concrete aids — slices of cake, measuring spoons, rulers, fraction puzzle pieces — to help your child "see" these concepts.

Money

Money concepts can be taught in a variety of ways. Children especially enjoy having and using their own money in practice sessions and games — as long as you promise to give it all back at the end!   Here are some ideas to try with your child:

▶ Give your child an allowance and have him or her open a savings account.

▶ Play *Monopoly* — a great favorite among even young children. As their grasp of basic math concepts improves, they can be allowed to act as the Banker.

▶ Practice making change. Start by teaching your child to "count up" from the cost of the item being purchased (at a real store or a "pretend store"). Children should learn to count up to coin amounts first, then to single dollars, and finally to multiple dollar bills. Following are tips for teaching these skills:

  • If the cost ends in a number other than 5 or 0, use pennies until you reach a number that ends with 5 or 0.

  • If the cost ends in 5 or a 0, use nickels and dimes until you reach 25, 50, or 75.

  • If the cost ends in 25, 50, or 75, use quarters until you reach 100 (one dollar).

You can also use money to begin teaching an older child about percentages. Toys are usually taxed. Help your child figure out the actual cost of a toy he or she wants to purchase by estimating the tax that will be added at the checkout counter. For example: "The car you want costs $4.75. The tax is 5 percent — that's 5 cents added to every dollar. $4.75 is almost $5. 5 dollars times 5 cents equals 25 cents. Now add that to $4.75. The real price of your car will be just about $5.00." For more practice making change, play *Shopping Lists* Games I and II. For more information about *Shopping Lists*, see page 112.

Time

Children develop a sense of time as they grow.   A young child initially perceives no difference between a week and a year. (The day following one birthday, they're likely to ask how soon they can expect the next.) This is one reason why children have so little patience when it comes to waiting for anticipated events. Anything more distant than tomorrow seems impossibly far away.

▶ Have your child mark off days on a calendar. He or she will gradually come to understand how much time a week takes, and that's a step in the direction of comprehending the length of a month and even a year.

▶ Be sure to have at least one non-digital (analog) clock in the house. If your clock has a second hand, that's even better. The movement of a second hand is something a child can see.

▶ Buy your child a toy clock or a non-digital watch, then teach him or her to tell time in the following sequence: hour, half-hour, quarter-hour, and finally five- and then one-minute intervals. Gradually introduce the different terms for the same concepts: "three-thirty" (easier) and "half past three" (harder), "four forty-five" (easier) and "a quarter to five" (harder). Pay special attention to troublesome areas. For example, children have a tendency to read 7:50 as 8:50 because the hour hand is closer to the 8 than the 7.

Geometry and measurement

Again, use concrete aids. To a child, seeing is believing, and touching is even more convincing.

▶ Have your child build a birdhouse or other object that requires accurate measurement and may also necessitate an understanding of perimeter, area, and other concepts.

▶ Let your child plot his or her growth on a wall chart (or make pencil marks along a doorjamb).

▶ Invite your child to help you make cookies. He or she can read the recipe, assist with measuring out dry ingredients, read the marks on the butter wrapper, and lick the spoon.

We could list dozens more suggestions — having your child read his or her weight on a scale, giving your child responsibility for reading the temperature on the thermometer each morning before school (and dressing accordingly), using tools, and so on. Draw on your own imagination and the tasks of your daily life to come up with others that will interest your child.

Incidentally, it's a *very* good idea to teach metric along with English measures (English measures being the ones Americans normally use: foot, inch, ounce, pound, etc.). The metric system is the standard in most countries, and while an effort to educate the American public (through road signs showing both miles and kilometers, for example) has largely been ignored, your child will probably need to know both.

How to help your child with word problems

The purpose of most word problems is to apply math concepts to "real-life" situations.   Many children have a hard time puzzling through the prose to find the numbers they need. The "SIR RIGHT" method can help, although some steps will be unnecessary for some problems. Teach it by modeling it for your child with one or more homework problems.

1. Start by reading the problem silently to get a general understanding of it.

2. Identify all numbers written as digits or words. It may be necessary to look for "hidden" numbers ("dozen," "one half as many," and so on).

3. Read the problem again, this time out loud, and draw a picture or diagram of it. (Some children may be able to do this in their heads.)

4. Read the problem yet again to find out what it is asking for. The answer may involve working backward from the question. (As many children have discovered, it's easier to solve a maze by starting at the Finish.)

5. Inquire, "What do I have to do to answer the problem?" Remember to add or multiply if a larger number is expected, or to subtract or divide if a smaller number is expected. Look for key words that tell you which operation is correct. For example:

    • "Total," "in all," and "altogether" indicate the need for addition or multiplication.

    • "How much is left," "how many are left," "how many more/greater/less than," and "how much older than" indicate the need for subtraction.

    • "How much...each" and "how many...each" indicate the need for division.

6. Give the problem smaller numbers than the ones actually used in it, and repeat steps 4 and 5 (if you are still puzzled by it).

7. Ham it up, acting out the problem if necessary.

8. Take a pencil and solve the problem, check your computation, and make sure that the answer makes sense.

Of course, you can also use real-life situations to make word problems more attractive to your child. Instead of asking, "If Johnny has two bananas and four friends to share them with, what should he do?", give your child two bananas the next time four friends come over and have him or her figure it out.

Finally, have your child make up word problems of interest to him or her. Research has shown that this helps students solve word problems on standardized tests.

HELP!

"My son simply cannot solve word problems. Other than that, his math homework is fine. He can read the problems, but if more than one computation process is required, he's lost."

Teach him the "SIR RIGHT" method explained above. Work through it with him until he is able to act independently.

"My daughter is a poor reader and has trouble with word problems as a result. Should I read them out loud to her?"

It would be wise to discuss this with the teacher. If the teacher approves, you can read the problems to your daughter so that she will not miss out on math concepts because of her reading difficulties. The teacher may be willing to make special arrangements for her during tests involving word problems.

"My son is a sixth grader who usually has no trouble with math. But she is having problems understanding and using the metric system. I don't understand it very well myself. How can I help?"

If you are not familiar with the metric system, take this opportunity to learn it with your child. The relationships within the metric system are easy to follow because they are based on the decimal system.

The units of length, weight, and capacity are the *meter*, *gram*, and *liter*, respectively. The prefixes *deci-*, *centi-* and *milli-* refer to 1/10, 1/100, and 1/1,000 of a unit. The prefixes *deca-*, *hecto-*, and *kilo-* refer to 10, 100, and 1,000 units.

Your son may be having trouble making mental images of metric measurements. Most people, when they think about a gallon, picture a gallon of milk. Help your son come up with similar images for the metric system. For example:

▶ A centimeter may be about the size of the fingernail on his thumb.

▶ A meter is about 1 yard.

▶ A liter is a little more than a quart, or half the size of a large-size bottle of Coca-Cola.

▶ A gram is about the weight of a large paper clip.

Comparative images like these will be most effective if your son is the one who originates them.

6

How To Help Your Child With Science and Social Studies

Definition of Science: "The attempt to find in the complexity of nature something which is simple and beautiful."
— Jacob Bronowski

Beyond the three R's

Learning how to learn about science and social studies requires completely different strategies than those needed for reading, writing, and arithmetic — the three R's considered basic to education. Yet success in science and social studies depends on how well your child has mastered those skills.

Some children who breeze through the three R's have difficulty with science and social studies. This may be due to a lack of interest, or it may depend on how comfortable a child feels with the way science and social studies texts are written and organized. It isn't uncommon for children to perform differently in each subject area. In other words, if your child is brilliant in math, don't assume that he or she will be equally brilliant in science. (That's equivalent to telling someone, "You can type, so you should be able to play the piano.")

How to help your child with "read-the-chapter, answer-the-questions" assignments

As early as third grade, children may be required to read chapters in science or social studies books and answer the questions following the chapters. (Or the teacher may substitute or supplement with other questions.) For children who are accustomed to reading primarily fiction — whether children's literature or the stories in their basal readers — this may prove to be a tedious task.

Reading informational material takes a whole new approach. Among other differences, it requires reading for *facts* as well as *theme*, and reading more *slowly* so as not to miss anything important. Informational material tends to be written more densely and may be written at a higher reading level than fiction intended for the same grade. And, frankly, it's often not written very well. It may be grammatically accurate but not very "considerate" of the reader.

The usual purpose of "read-the-chapter, answer-the-questions" exercises is to train children to study a body of information for testing at a later date. The following strategy is designed to help your child become comfortable with this process. Start by reading it aloud to your child (including the CAUTION at the end) and modeling it until he or she gains confidence and proficiency.

1. **Preview the chapter.**

   Skim through it quickly before actually starting to read it. Previewing means:

   • reading the chapter headings and subheadings,

   • reading the introduction,

   • reading the summary at the end,

   • looking at graphs, tables, charts, maps, and other illustrations, and

   • checking out features like the index and the glossary, which may guide you to some of the answers you need to find.

Previewing helps you budget your reading time by giving you an idea of how long the chapter is and whether you are familiar with the subject matter.

If the chapter is long, you may want to read it in more than one sitting. If it contains many new and difficult words, chunk it into small pieces and tackle them one at a time.

(PARENTS: These steps may need some advance preparation. For example, your child may ignore the legend at the bottom of a chart or a map and misunderstand it entirely. Or your child may not understand the purpose of the index or glossary. You may want to begin by paging through the book, pointing out the various parts and explaining them in simple language.)

2. **Now read the questions.**

   Read them all the way through, looking up any words you don't understand.

3. **Now read the chapter carefully.**

4. **Now answer the questions, looking back through the chapter whenever you need to.**

   If you are supposed to write the answers in complete sentences, be sure to check your capitalization and punctuation.

   (PARENTS: If your child needs help checking his or her work, use all or part of the A-OK method described on pages 64 - 65.)

CAUTION

DON'T, repeat DON'T get in the habit of using the "search-and-destroy" approach to these assignments. In other words, DON'T read the questions first and then skim the chapter to find the answers. If you don't give the chapter a THOROUGH reading, you may miss important facts and concepts you need for tests.

HELP!

"My daughter is not in the highest reading group in her class, but she still has to use the same science book they use. There is no way that she can complete her assignments by herself; her reading skills aren't up to it. Should I help by reading the chapters out loud to her?"

If the text is really too difficult for her, talk to the teacher. If the teacher insists that your daughter participate with the rest of the class in using this text, it may be necessary for you to read the chapters to her.

"My son always gets A's on his daily work in history, but he rarely passes the tests. How can he answer questions correctly on his daily work but not remember the answers for tests?"

He may be using the "search-and-destroy" method to answer the questions in his daily work. Encourage your son to read the chapter carefully BEFORE trying to answer the questions. A quick review the night or morning before the test will help, too.

"My son never reads his geography chapter before starting to answer the questions at the end. Yet he seems to get all the answers right, and he also does well on tests. Should I still insist that he read the chapters carefully?"

Talk to the teacher. It may be that he or she lectures right from the text or allows class time for reading the chapters. On the other hand, your son may simply be familiar with the material being covered. As long as he's doing such a good job, let him continue in the same manner. (Remember the old saying: "If it isn't broken, don't fix it!") Keep an eye on him, though, when he gets other teachers whose teaching style may make it necessary for your son to do more work on his own.

How to help your child study chapters for tests

Knowing how to study chapters for tests is vital, since your child will be required to do this through high school and beyond. Relatively few children can read a chapter once and retain all the information needed for a test; most need to practice more intense study methods. Look back at pages 23 - 25 for suggestions that can help you help your child. Following are more techniques for you to try.

▶ If studying for a test has been preceded by a "read-the-chapter, answer-the-questions" exercise, half of the work has been done already. If not, the study session should begin with a preview and a careful reading of the chapter. See pages 86 - 87.

▶ Even if your child has carefully read the whole chapter once, a methodical rereading may be necessary to prepare for a test. Here is the procedure we recommend:

1. Have your child read each paragraph or section, then stop.

2. Now have your child try to project one or two questions the teacher might possibly ask about the paragraph or section.

3. Record these questions on individual notecards (flashcards), with the answers on the back.

4. After your child has finished rereading the entire chapter, make additional flashcards for any questions at the end of the chapter which cannot be answered immediately.

5. Finally, make flashcards for new vocabulary words introduced in the chapter.

Once these first five steps have been accomplished, the *real* studying can begin.

6. Go over the flashcards until your child knows the answers automatically. Given enough drill-and-practice, his or her memory should "kick in" even if test anxiety sets in.

7. If you know what format the test will take — matching, fill-in-the-blanks, short answer, and so on — try to construct a sample test with your child. (This can be especially beneficial for children who have high test anxiety.)

This process takes time and commitment on your part and your child's. But our experience as students, teachers, and tutors has convinced us that it *works* — and often results in improved grades.

Making it fun

Studying for tests will *not* be fun if you and your child start too late. From the very first day of the new school year, emphasize to your child that he or she *must* let you know about a test as soon as it is announced in class. (You may want to use the Assignment Sheet on page 139 or 141 to record test dates and relevant information.) Once you hear about a test, you and your child can plan your study time accordingly.

Many games can be adapted to studying for chapter tests. See chapter 8 for suggestions.

HELP!

"There is NO WAY that my son can make up sample test questions. He has a hard enough time just reading the chapter, much less understanding it well enough to invent questions."

Your son needs you to model this for him. Start by reading the chapter with him, paragraph by paragraph. Then have your son make up a question while you make one up at the same time. Record the questions on flashcards. Don't expect miracles overnight, but your son should gradually become familiar enough with the kinds of questions his teacher asks that he can begin constructing his own.

"My daughter can understand chapter material fairly easily, but her attention span is very short. The night before a test, she is in misery studying the chapters. The chapters are just too long."

Your daughter needs to study well in advance of a test — not only the night before. As soon as a chapter is assigned, have her chunk it into smaller portions, then read and study one portion a night. This eliminates the last-minute cramming routine that most children find frustrating and scary.

"My daughter never needs to study for tests. The most she ever has to do is quickly read over a chapter the night before. I'm afraid that when she encounters more difficult material in college, she will fall apart. Shouldn't she form the habit NOW of studying more carefully?"

Her manner of studying may carry her through college and beyond. However, it isn't uncommon for outstanding high-school students to run into trouble later, when they are asked to master more difficult materials. If your daughter is serious about her grades, you may want to enroll her in a study skills course so she will be ready to adjust her study habits if and when this becomes necessary.

How to help your child with graphics

Much of the material in science and social studies texts is presented in the form of maps, charts, timelines, and graphs. Formal instruction in graphics other than maps typically begins in the third grade and continues through junior high school; it may be included as part of the math, reading, science, and/or social studies curriculum. Even so, some children continue to have difficulty interpreting graphics or fail to see their importance. This is especially true if reading is a chore for them. They concentrate so hard on the text that they don't have any energy left over for the graphics.

Map-reading skills may be introduced as early as kindergarten. Instruction usually begins with the concepts of "near/far," "up/down," and "above/below" and gradually moves to complex concepts like the International Date Line, map scale, and map projection/distortion. (These are normally covered by the sixth grade.) Often map concepts take root slowly and are hard for children to grasp. Many third-grade students, for example, are amazed to learn that we do not live "inside" the earth. Others regularly confuse cities with states and continents with countries.

A good way to help your child understand graphic materials is by helping him or her to make maps, graphs, timelines, and so on with construction paper, crayons, colorful markers, rulers, and other interesting tools. Hands-on experience is not only fun; it also enables children to comprehend the reasons for graphics and the ways they are produced.

Helping your child read maps

▶ Find out the sequence of map skills taught in your child's class. If your child is experiencing difficulty, perhaps he or she has not mastered prerequisite skills. Ask the teacher for suggestions you can use at home.

▶ Many children have trouble with the concept of distance. One of us tutored a 10-year-old whose longest on-the-ground "trip" was a five-mile ride from his home to the airport. The idea of driving 100 miles in a car was beyond his comprehension. You can instill a sensitivity to distance with activities like these:

  • Walk a mile with your child, then show how a mile is represented on a map.

- Ask your child to keep track of the odometer reading during car trips. (If you have a "trip meter," set it to 0 at the beginning for an exact count of the miles traveled.) Then show how that distance is represented on a road map.

▶ Orient your child to the four cardinal directions. Go outside and point out north, south, east, and west. If you have a compass, use it to demonstrate direction. (You may want to buy your child a compass of his or her own; kids love gadgets like these.) Be patient when helping your child to learn these concepts.

▶ Relative location — the location of one place in relation to another — can also be difficult for children to grasp. An effective lead-up activity is to construct a number/dot board like the one shown below.

$$
\begin{array}{cccc}
1 & 2 & 3 & 4 \\
\cdot & \cdot & \cdot & \cdot \\
5 & 6 & 7 & 8 \\
\cdot & \cdot & \cdot & \cdot \\
9 & 10 & 11 & 12 \\
\cdot & \cdot & \cdot & \cdot
\end{array}
$$

Using the board, ask your child a series of questions like these:

- What direction is dot 6 from dot 10?

- Is dot 7 north or south of dot 11?

- If you were going from dot 8 to dot 7, in what direction would you be going?

▶ Encourage your child to read a map legend carefully before attempting to answer any questions about the map.

▶ Determine the meaning of any other symbols on the map and help your child discover how and where they are used.

▶ Refresh your own knowledge of map-related vocabulary. Your child may be asked to locate a continent, a peninsula, or a strait on a map without having any inkling of what those terms mean.

▶ Keep an atlas and a globe at home (perhaps in your child's study center) and use them frequently — to add meaning to coin and stamp collections, when reading stories about other lands, and so on.

CAUTION

If your child is colorblind, he or she may have special difficulty with color-coded maps. Be sure that the teacher is aware of this condition early in the school year.

Helping your child read graphs, diagrams, and tables

Graphs, diagrams, and tables are common graphics. The following tips can help you help your child to use these aids:

▶ Identify the title of the graphic and discuss what information is being illustrated.

▶ When working with a graph, start by identifying what kind it is: line graph, bar graph, pie graph, or pictograph. Examples of each are shown on page 94.

▶ Read line graphs, bar graphs, pictographs, tables, and charts from the "outside in." In other words, look first at any headings at the top, the bottom, and along both sides before moving to the information contained in the graphic.

▶ When working with a graph or a timeline, identify the unit of measure used (inch or foot or mile, day or week or month or year, quantity, etc.).

▶ When working with a diagram, determine how it is labeled. For example, a skeleton may have labels for each bone.

▶ Determine the meanings of any symbols on the graphic.

▶ Discuss ways in which the graphic can be used. For example, a graphic of toy sales before and after Christmas can help store owners decide how many toys to stock up on each month and how many cash registers to keep open. An airplane schedule is a table used by airport employees, passengers, and persons taking passengers to or from the airport.

▶ Take turns with your child inventing questions that can be answered by studying the graphic.

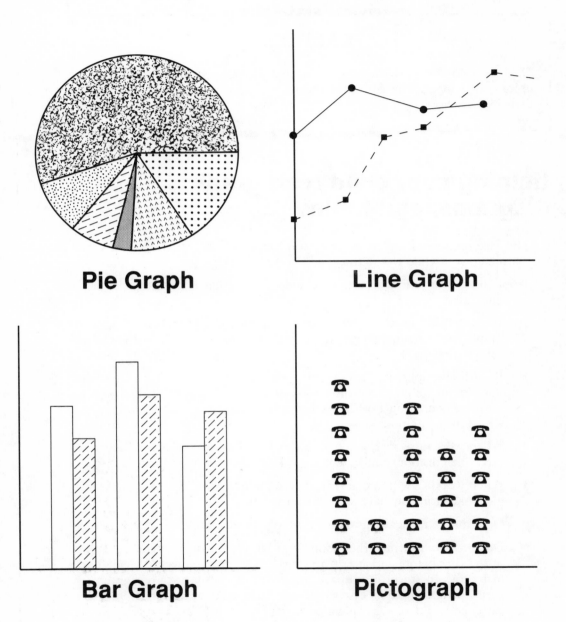

Pie Graph

Line Graph

Bar Graph

Pictograph

Making it fun

▶ Play games that stress geography and graphic skills mastery. See page 117 for suggestions.

▶ Develop "graphics radar." Both you and your child can keep an eye out for graphics, then discuss them together. The national newspaper, *USA Today,* is an excellent resource for clear, colorful maps, charts, and graphs of all kinds.

▶ If your child is a sports fan, keep a map handy so he or she can locate the home cities of favorite teams. When watching sports events, keep a map or a globe handy for locating the countries, cities, and continents mentioned during the competition.

▶ If your child is an animal fancier, locate the countries and continents that are the original homes of his or her favorite animals. On trips to the zoo, take a small world map along for the same purpose.

▶ When planning a family trip, help your child to locate your destination on a map. If you are going by plane, discuss how long it would take to get there by car. When touring a city, locate points of interest on a city map (available from most Boards of Tourism or Information offices or kiosks)

▶ Send away for a map of your child's favorite amusement or theme park. Learning map reading skills is fun when the map is colorful and exciting.

▶ Purchase a large, colorful map of the world and hang it on a wall in your child's room or study center.

▶ Most shopping malls provide centrally-located maps of their stores and shops. The next time you go shopping with your child, lead him or her to one of these maps. Then let your child lead *you* from one store to another.

▶ Many children enjoy keeping behavior charts on a daily basis. Let your child construct his or her own chart for tracking chores done, home-work completed, numbers of books read, math facts mastered, and so on. Record progress with checkmarks or stickers.

▶ Make a "pedigree chart" showing the lineage of your family, or make a family timeline. (These can also be nice gifts for relatives.)

HELP!

"My son is in the fifth grade. His next science test is going to be on the human skeletal system. His teacher is going to give him a diagram of the skeleton, and he will have to label the bones. How can I help him prepare?"

Make multiple photocopies of a *clear* picture or drawing of a skeleton and have your son practice writing in the correct name for each bone. It may take many repetitions before he knows them all (which is the reason behind the need for multiple photocopies), so be patient and encouraging. If you can come up with any mnemonics or "memory tricks" (for example, "Elvis the pelvis"), so much the better.

"My daughter got a D on her last social studies test. She told me that she had read the chapter carefully and didn't understand why her grade was so low. We looked over the questions she missed and discovered that the information she needed to know was in the chapter, but it was presented in charts and time-lines rather than text. My daughter claims that she 'skipped those parts' because she didn't think they were important."

This is not at all uncommon. Many children perceive graphics as "free spaces" in reading and simply advance to the next paragraph. Communicate to your daughter the importance of graphic information, using the suggestions given on pages 91 - 95.

"My son never has trouble reading graphs, diagrams, or maps of any kind. How can I encourage him to develop this talent further?"

Why not name him the "Official Navigator" on family vacations? This will give him the opportunity to put his skills to work in real-life situations. Allow him plenty of time in advance to study the maps you will be using. If he is responsible for reading them under pressure or during times of peak traffic, or if he makes an error and *you* take a wrong turn, you'll both get frustrated.

You can also encourage your son to include graphics in his school reports and projects. Creating graphics may be time-consuming (especially without the aid of computer graphics software), but they add that "something extra" that children enjoy — and teachers often reward.

How to build your child's fund of general information

Children who have a rich fund of general information and background knowledge on a variety of subjects will find science and social studies (and reading and writing) easier and more interesting than those who do not. As a caring parent, you have the privilege and the responsibility of sharing the world with your child.

Describe your own childhood experiences, the things that interested you then (and interest you now), your favorite places, and whatever else occurs to you. Be ready at a moment's notice to answer questions that occur to your child — or promise to help your child find the answers if you don't know them yourself. Talk, talk, talk — about feelings, hobbies, politics, advertisements, TV shows, music, roller skates, road signs, poems, movies, grandparents, pets, anything and everything! And listen, listen, listen to your child.

A child who's treated as someone worth talking to develops a sense of value and self-respect. A child who's treated as someone worth listening to develops strong verbal skills and an undying curiosity. And both of you together develop better communication and a better understanding of each other's wants and needs, hopes and dreams, personalities and beings. The more you converse with each other, the more rewarding your conversations and your relationship will become.

Here are a few suggestions for stimulating activities to enjoy with your child. Talk about them before; talk about them during; talk about them after.

▶ Have your child watch TV news and documentaries.

▶ When renting or buying videos for home viewing, include educational tapes.

▶ Take your child to natural history museums, science museums, art museums, children's museums, zoos, botanical gardens, historical sites, and more.

▶ Take your child to national parks and forests and go on tours with the rangers.

▶ Have your child read articles in a newspaper or in news magazines, or read them aloud to him or her.

▶ Take *frequent* trips to the public library. (Jim Trelease, the author of *The Read-Aloud Handbook*, asks parents to think about their priorities by comparing the number of times they take their kids to the library vs. the number of times they take them to the shopping mall.) If your child is mature enough and has developed library skills, you can go to the library together and arrange to meet in a certain place at a certain time (an hour later, for example). Then let your child have the run of the place.

One child we know was eagerly scanning microfiche when he was still too short to reach it without standing on a chair. And he knew from an early age how to ask librarians for directions and suggestions. His idea of a "fun night out" was an evening spent at the library!

▶ Make vacations learning experiences. Read travel guides together and let your child participate in the where-to-go, what-to-see decision-making process.

▶ Watch *quality* movies with your child, then discuss them afterward. Don't just limit your choices to commercial theaters. Check out movies offered at libraries, museums, and other cultural centers. And don't just limit your choices to current movies. If you have a VCR, use it to screen old comedies, historical dramas, westerns, and adventures.

▶ Plan "theme" birthday parties with your child that involve some research. For example: an American Revolution costume party; an Inventor's Convention; a play.

▶ Take advantage of every "teachable moment" that presents itself during the course of a normal day: trips to the grocery store, gardening, walks around the block, meal preparation, dinnertime discussions, and many, many more.

Remember: your child is eager to learn. And you are your child's most important teacher.

7

How To Help Your Child With Foreign Languages, Projects, Reports, and Papers

"Deadlines are liberating."
— William F. Buckley, Jr.

How to help your child with homework in foreign languages

During the elementary years, foreign languages are taught primarily for enrichment purposes. Instruction is typically designed to give children a "taste" of a foreign language so they will want to enroll in more formal courses in junior high school, high school, and college. In most cases, the foreign language teacher is a specialist who visits the elementary classroom once, twice, or more often during the week. The curriculum varies greatly.

If your child is given the opportunity to receive foreign language instruction, start by finding out about the program. How often will it meet? How intensive will it be? What kinds of things will your child be learning? Will homework be required? If so, what can you do to help at home?

Like one's native language, a foreign language is learned more by practice and "absorption" than by any conscious effort to master the rules of grammar. (In any event, these come later, not in the elementary curriculum.) Your child's practice can be aided by television, videocassettes, audiocassettes, records, foreign language clubs, and pen pals. Naturally, the preferred way to learn a language is to live in a country where it is spoken, but this is not an option for most young children. If you're planning a foreign vacation anyway, you may want to consider visiting a country where your child can hear the language he or she is studying.

An important point to remember when helping your child with a foreign language is *not to overcorrect*. Children who are learning English are allowed to experiment — for example, with "ed" as the past tense form of all verbs, including "runned." Children who are learning a foreign language should be given the same leeway.

Making it fun

Learning about other cultures can be fascinating. Read to your child about life in the country or countries where people speak the language he or she is learning. Seek out articles in *National Geographic* and travel magazines (the more pictures, the better). Volunteer to assist with International Fairs at your child's school. Obtain posters and other small items from travel agents or import shops. If you have friends from that country, ask them if they wouldn't mind spending some time talking to your child. Visit a local restaurant that specializes in foods of the country. Use your imagination!

Try using games, especially if you can speak the language. Work with your child to make flashcards of the words your child is learning. Since most of these will have to do with animals, foods, colors, people, and actions, make word-and-picture cards for playing Concentration (see pages 122 - 123) or Wet Cat (a game similar to "Old Maid"). Use a trivia board game, making up cards to teach vocabulary from the language and facts about the countries where it is spoken.

HELP!

"My daughter is a good student and is taking Spanish in school. However, she isn't at all motivated to practice the phrases she's assigned for homework."

Talk with the teacher to determine the reason for your daughter's "couldn't care less" attitude. She may be afraid to take risks, which studying a foreign language certainly demands. She may be hesitant to pronounce the new words for fear of being ridiculed. Or she may be finding that foreign languages do not come as easily to her as other subjects.

Start by relaxing any demands you are currently making on her to "do well" in her Spanish class. Instead, emphasize the value and fun of learning a new language. Make an effort to learn the words she is being taught so the two of you can have mini-conversations. She may feel more encouraged to take risks if you show that *you* are.

If these approaches are unsuccessful, it may be wise to let your daughter discontinue her Spanish instruction until she is older and perhaps more interested. Although some aspects of language learning are easier when one is very young, this is not true for all aspects. Plus learning is easier when motivation is higher. Instead of spoiling any desire your daughter might have to learn a foreign language in the future, let it go for now.

"My son has difficulty reading in English, and now he's also being taught to read in French. Will this cause a problem?"

Knowledge of two languages generally promotes conceptual development in both, and this development is directly related to reading skills. So studying French shouldn't hurt your son. However, if he continues to have a hard time reading English, he should take a second language only if the emphasis is on speaking it rather than reading it.

"My son is excited about learning French and is picking up oral French easily. But he has problems reading in French, and this prevents him from completing his homework."

Your son is mastering the most difficult aspect of the new language, for which he should be praised and encouraged. You might want to find out whether his teacher or an advanced student could provide his homework on an audiotape so he can read and listen simultaneously. Some of the suggestions for improving reading skills found in chapter 3 might also be helpful here.

"My daughter does well on her weekly Spanish quizzes, but she has difficulty with tests that cover several units. It seems that while she's learning the material in one unit, she's forgetting everything she learned before."

Your daughter needs to review previous lessons on a regular basis. Learning a foreign language is a cumulative process; you can't just learn the new and "dump" the old. You can help her to review by adapting the suggestions found on pages 88 - 89.

"My son studies with a friend every evening. They practice their Spanish together, but neither uses a very good Spanish accent. Should I let them continue?"

Be glad that your son is practicing and progressing without your overt assistance. The only help you should offer is to provide videocassettes, audiocassettes, or records to expand their practice. In time, their accent should improve.

How to help your child with special projects

Art Fair, Science Fair, social studies displays! Special projects are a welcome diversion from daily ditto sheets and textbook assignments — but they can also be a nightmare for parents. If your child doesn't quite know what to do or how to do it, *you* could end up bearing the burden.

There is a solution to more child participation and less parental involvement: *planning*. As soon as the assignment is made, you and your child should meet to discuss it and plot out a project plan. This checklist can get you started. A worksheet version suitable for photocopying is found on pages 169 - 170.

☐ 1. Decide on the project theme.

☐ 2. Have the theme approved by the teacher.

☐ 3. Make a list of things that need to be done and the order in which they should be completed.

☐ 4. Decide who is going to do what.

☐ 5. Set deadlines for completion of each part of the project.

☐ 6. Make a list of the materials needed.

☐ 7. Make a projected budget.

☐ 8. Send away for resource materials needed.

☐ 9. Contact community resources.

☐ 10. Visit the library.

☐ 11. Complete the project on schedule.

Special projects can be fun, *if* children are allowed to choose themes that interest them, and *if* they are encouraged (not smothered) by parental supervision. As you work with your child, lend your support when it is needed and when it is asked for. Avoid the temptation to do the project for your child. Great joy can be found in a job well done — and independently done.

HELP!

"My daughter doesn't have any ideas for her science experiment. I have no idea what is appropriate and what isn't. Where can we go to get ideas?"

Look around you. You may find inspiration in the kitchen for experiments on heat, refrigeration, or decay. You may find inspiration in the garden for experiments on plant or insect development. For additional ideas, talk to a librarian — or a friendly scientist in your community.

"Last year my son was supposed to make a social studies display, but I did all the work. I refuse to do it again this year. What can I do to get him involved?"

Follow the checklist above. Decide first what needs to be done, then who is going to do it. Because you are trying to limit your involvement, confine your contributions to tasks like providing transportation to the library, proofreading a first draft, or supplying opportunities for your son to earn money to cover the cost of the project. See page 171 for an "Agreement Form" the two of you can use to formalize your arrangement.

"My son simply cannot draw. Last year his social studies poster was a disaster! Should I do it for him this year?"

If your son is truly embarrassed by his inability to draw, perhaps his teacher can suggest another format for the poster. For example, if you have access to a computer graphics program (and it's one your son can learn to use), this may be the solution.

"Last year at our school the Science Fair mostly consisted of parent projects. My daughter completed her project all by herself, and it was obviously not as polished as the others. Should I help her more this year?"

Independence is the primary goal of any special project. If your daughter is content to complete her project on her own, more power to her. Be available to serve as a resource, but continue to foster her independent spirit. In other words, hands off!

How to help your child with book reports

With the threat of illiteracy looming all about us, teachers are encouraging students to read, read, and read some more. It is not unusual for elementary school children to be required to complete a book a week, or (in upper grades) a longer, more substantial book a month.

As a caring parent, you can uphold this excellent emphasis on reading by taking regular trips to the library or bookstore with your child, and by planning regular family reading times. Given the choice, most children will opt to rent the video or buy the audiotape over reading the book. Don't give the choice. Insist that multimedia aids be used as supplements rather than substitutes for the real thing.

In many classrooms today, the formal book report is a thing of the past. Instead, children are required to complete alternate assignments to give evidence of having read a book. Posters, puppets, and plays have supplanted written reports, with some teachers devising a variety of creative options. Many teachers who still assign book reports provide a format for children to follow.

If your child is assigned a book report, and if the teacher does not provide a format, the outlines on pages 173 - 184 can serve as frameworks for writing reports on three different kinds of books: fiction, nonfiction, and biography.

A book report is generally perceived as something to slog through. (You probably don't have especially fond memories from your own childhood where book reports are concerned.) They may not be the most fascinating and stimulating of all assignments, but they do serve a variety of purposes. They get children reading, and they get them reading *carefully.* If children know that they're going to have to write about something they read, they're less likely to skim it. A good book-report format also trains a child to pay attention to details like setting, characters, and plot.

The most critical factor in making a book report more bearable is finding a proper match between a book and a child. Help your child select a book that is both interesting and readable. Ask your school or public librarian for suggestions. Find out if the teacher has a list of books he or she especially recommends.

If your child is assigned a book and is not given the luxury of choosing, help him or her plan enough time to complete it. Work reading assignments into your child's homework schedule or incorporate them into your family reading time.

HELP!

"My son is required to hand in a book report every other week. It's always a hassle. The night before the report is due, we're always pushing to get it done. Isn't this too severe an assignment for a fifth grader?"

If the book report is always being done the night before it's due, then it *is* a severe assignment — for you and your family. Help your son select books that are interesting to him and are written at a comfortable level of difficulty. Then help him to establish a reading schedule that enables him to complete his reading early. Two nights before the report is due, encourage him to write a rough draft. Work with him to proofread it and find and correct any errors. The night before the report is due, he can complete the final draft — a much easier and more manageable task than starting cold.

"My daughter is assigned a book a month. She is required to read the book and then take an in-class test based on her reading. She has failed every test. This month the assigned book is **Johnny Tremain**. *She claims that she can't understand the book and wants to rent the video instead."*

If the book is extremely difficult for your daughter to read, viewing the video may enable her to grasp the basic story line. *Watch it with her* — well in advance of when the test is scheduled. Then encourage her to read one chapter of the book at a time and discuss it with you. Use the Book Report Outlines on pages 173 - 176 to help her study for the test.

"My daughter loves to read but hates to write reports. She'll talk about a book forever, but writing a report is sheer torture. How can I help make this task more tolerable for her?"

Use the outlines on pages 173 - 184 to provide structure. Following a format greatly simplifies report writing. If your daughter likes to talk about a book she has just read, encourage her to talk into a recorder while following one of the outlines. When she finishes, she can transcribe her oral report into written form.

"My son would rather read than eat. He reads many more books than required by his teacher, and he writes well-developed book reports. Should I be concerned about his preoccupation with reading?"

Only if he is using reading as a substitute for real-life activities or relationships. If his life is balanced — if he also participates in school activities, plays with friends, and pursues non-book interests — then celebrate the fact that he has formed such a good habit at such a young age.

How to help your child with term papers

Helping your child with a written report may bring flashbacks of your own late nights spent hunched over a typewriter in a dormitory room. Grinding out a report at the last minute is nobody's idea of fun. Fortunately, your child can learn from *you* the benefits of advance planning.

Often children are assigned a report without receiving any instruction on how to go about doing it. Or they may not be taught how to use instruction given previously. For example, children may learn how to outline in a language arts class, but may not be shown how to apply this skill to a term paper for a social studies class. Even if they are told what to do, they may never have seen a sample of a finished report. In other words, they may have no idea what is expected of them.

Planning is the key to a successful paper-writing experience. *You* may have gotten by on all-nighters, but it's your duty as a caring parent to help your child develop healthier habits. With patience and guidance from you, he or she can learn to live with a far more organized and efficient schedule. This checklist can get you started. An expanded version suitable for photocopying is found on pages 185 - 186.

☐ 1. Make sure that the assignment is understood.

☐ 2. Find out all the requirements and specifications for the paper. For example: Will it need a title page? A table of contents? A bibliography?

Pictures, illustrations, maps, or other graphics? Should it be typed or can it be handwritten?

- ☐ 3. Decide on a topic.
- ☐ 4. Have the topic approved by the teacher.
- ☐ 5. Research the topic in the library.
- ☐ 6. Contact community resources related to the topic.
- ☐ 7. Write letters needed to obtain information from national sources.
- ☐ 8. Take notes on the materials found or obtained.
- ☐ 9. Develop an outline.
- ☐ 10. Write a rough draft.
- ☐ 11. Proofread the rough draft using the A-OK method. (See pages 64 - 65 for a description of this method.)
- ☐ 12. Write the final draft.

Work with your child to set a deadline for each step of this checklist. Decide what he or she can do independently and where you will need to help. Our experience has shown that the most difficult steps are notetaking, outlining, and writing the rough draft. A child about to do his or her first report will probably need a great deal of guidance and support.

HELP!

"My daughter, a fourth grader, has been assigned a term paper on Norway. She did a report on volleyball last month and got a C. Her teacher was upset that she copied from the encyclopedia. My daughter has no idea how to write a report."

If the teacher is requiring her to write a report with no formal instruction, your assistance is much needed. Don't write the report *for* her, but do help her to extract information from other resource and reference books in addition to encyclopedias and put it into her own words. Give her a copy of the checklist on pages 185 - 186 to guide her in planning the project.

Try to make this a positive experience by going to a travel agent for pictures and writing to various sources (for example, the Norwegian Embassy) for information. Your daughter will be writing reports for a long time, so anything you can do to instill a positive attitude will be extremely important.

"Last year my son wrote a term paper for school. He did a good job, but he waited until the night before to do most of the work. How can I help him budget his time better?"

Take him through the checklist on pages 102 - 103, assigning dates and deadlines to each step. Give him a copy of the checklist on pages 185 - 186 to use for his own reference. Work out a system of rewards for successful completion of each step.

"My son enjoys research and does a fine job of writing term papers for school. What can I do to let him know that I support his efforts — without interfering?"

When your son is researching a topic, communicate to him that you are interested in what he is doing. Let him share his findings at the dinner table. Keep your eyes and ears open for community resources which may enhance his research.

8
Playing Games

*"You can't teach a child unless
you reach him."*
— Unknown

The value of playing games
with your child

One of our friends grew up with five brothers and sisters. The expense of raising so many children left little money for movies and other "going-out" activities. Instead, her parents made sure that the house was stocked with games of all kinds — and all of the children grew up to be avid game-players. Although the primary intent may not have been educational, the end results certainly were. Our friend recalls learning how to spell over a *Scrabble* board, learning about money over *Monopoly*, and more while gathered around the table with her family.

The main reason to play games with your child is because it's *fun*. It's a wonderful opportunity for you to spend time together doing something you both enjoy. It's also a ready-made opportunity for you to reinforce basic concepts and skills.

In the context of doing homework, games can provide relief from the monotony and drudgery of drill-and-practice. (Almost any child would rather play Hangman than review a written spelling list.) This chapter includes suggestions for dozens of games you can buy or make yourself. Many can be used to help teach a variety of subjects.

"And the winner is..."

While recent years have seen the introduction of many non-competitive games (games where "everyone wins"), most still depend on *one* person emerging as winner. When you first play a game with your child that is new to him or her, it's almost a given that the winner will be you. Parents have asked us whether they should deliberately "lose" on occasion so their children won't be frustrated. We can't in good conscience recommend this. All children would rather win than lose, but most can tell the difference between *really* winning and winning because someone let them. Instead, try these strategies:

▶ When playing a game with your child, keep the focus on *self-competition*. Encourage your child to improve his or her level of achievement each time the game is played. (For example, your child could aim for a higher personal score or a faster time.)

▶ Explore several different types of games with your child. Look for one or more that he or she can eventually play well enough to win. (It's more fun for *you* when your child reaches this point.) You may find that your child has a gift for certain games; we know one third-grader who was beating his father at chess by age 6.

▶ Don't limit your choices to games of skill. Also include games of chance, where your child has the same likelihood of winning as you do. Young children enjoy *Candyland*, *Chutes and Ladders*, and other games where moves are determined by a spinner or a roll of the dice. These may not be appropriate for homework sessions since they don't teach much in the way of concepts or skills, but they are fine for other occasions.

When to play games with your child

Naturally you can play games during leisure time, "just for the fun of it," but games can also be incorporated into regular homework sessions. For example, instead of doing multiplication flashcards, you can play "Multiplication Baseball" instead. Draw a baseball field and let your child go from base to base with each fact he or she gets right. Points are scored for each home run.

▶ In most cases, games should be scheduled for the end of a homework session. ("When you finish all of your other work — neatly and completely — we'll play a game together.") The game can function as the "carrot" at the end of the homework "stick."

▶ If your child is a slow worker, this may not be the best approach. Many teachers permit students to play learning games only after their regular classwork is finished. A child who simply can't get everything done in time feels left out of the fun. You probably can't change the teacher's policy about this, but you can make up for it at home. Divide your child's homework into mini-sessions and play games in between.

▶ Use games frequently to provide the extra drill needed to overlearn information for a test. Children don't mind going over facts again and again if this involves an element of play. (At least, they don't mind as much.)

How to buy games to play with your child

Many commercial games are available through educational suppliers as well as regular toy stores, department stores, and catalogs. Their quality varies greatly. Be sure to examine a game carefully *before* purchasing it. You may not be able to open it if it is sealed, but directions are usually printed on the bottom of the box, and you can use these to determine whether a game is appropriate for your child's needs and skill level. Inquire about the company's return/refund policy at the time of purchase in case a particular game doesn't work out.

Here are some questions to guide your buying decision:

1. Does this game reinforce a specific skill or skills my child needs to master?

2. Do I have the time to make an inexpensive game that will do the job as effectively?

 If so, stop here and give it a try. If not, continue:

3. Is the game attractive and appealing in theme, color, and design?

4. Is the game well-constructed and durable?

5. Is the skill level appropriate for my child?

 Most games will indicate an *age* level — for example, "for ages 5 and up" — but this won't necessarily conform to your child's *skill* level. So this question will take some thought.

6. Are the directions clear and easy to follow?

7. How long does it take to complete the game? Is it too long or too short to fit the time period I have in mind?

8. How much actual drill-and-practice does the game involve?

Some supposedly "educational" games contain a lot of nonsense or distracting filler activities. These are okay for leisure play, but not for homework sessions.

9. Does the game enable a child to gauge his or her own progress in skill development? For example, with a trivia game, a child will know when he or she is improving.

10. Can the entire game, or parts of the game, be adapted for uses other than those specified by the manufacturer?

11. Is the game simple enough that my child can play it with siblings or friends and without a great deal of help from me?

And, finally:

12. Taking all of these factors into consideration, is the game worth the cost?

As you search store shelves and catalog pages for games appropriate for your child, you may feel overwhelmed by the sheer numbers available. Following are some tried-and-true favorites that come recommended by parents and children alike. See pages 117 - 118 for manufacturers' addresses in the event that you can't find these games in stores.

▶ *Yahtzee* (Milton Bradley), *'SMATH* (Pressman), and *Mille Bornes* (Parker Brothers) all provide practice in addition.

▶ *Boggle* (Parker Brothers), *Scrabble for Juniors* (Coleco), *Wordsearch* and *Wheel of Fortune* (both Pressman) all provide practice in spelling and vocabulary development. (*Wheel of Fortune*, if you don't already know, is simply a glorified version of Hangman.) *Pyramid* (Cardinal) provides practice with classifications.

▶ Practice in making change ($1 - $1,000) is provided by *Monopoly* (Parker Brothers) and *Shopping Lists Game I* ($0.01-$1) and *Shopping Lists Game II* ($0.01-$5) (DLM).

▶ Checkers, chess, and Chinese checkers provide practice in strategic thinking. For strategic thinking paired with geography skills, try *Risk* (Parker Brothers).

When playing any of these games — and others you choose — it's important to let your child participate in as many ways as possible. It may seem easier or more efficient for you to keep score or make change, but in the long run your child will benefit more if you let him or her assume these responsibilities.

Buying computer games

Shopping for computer games requires a different strategy than shopping for other types of games. One reason is because computer games tend to be more expensive. Another reason is because the copy on the box often doesn't tell you much about the game inside. With any computer game you are considering, it's always best to *try before you buy*.

▶ Start with your school or local public library. Many have computer games you can check out and sample at home.

▶ Ask your child which of his or her friends plays computer games at home. (Children usually know who has a home computer and who doesn't, since computers are so fascinating to them.) Then talk to the parents about the games. If possible, arrange a visit and personally preview the ones they recommend.

▶ Publications like *Family Computing*, *A+*, and *Electronic Learning* frequently review computer games. Time spent at the library can save you time spent talking to store clerks who may or may not know about the products.

▶ Shop at stores that specialize in computer software and hardware. Often they will have sample copies of games and computers you can try them out on. Some have liberal returns policies in case you buy a game and later decide that it isn't right for your child. In contrast, most department and discount stores will not allow returns of computer programs unless they are defective, and then they will only replace the program, not exchange it for a different one or refund your money.

Here are some questions to guide your buying decision:

1. Do we have all the special equipment needed to run this program?

   Check the requirements listed on the box. If you have to buy a joystick, a color monitor, or other equipment before the program will work on your computer, it may not be worth it. Then again, purchasing this new equipment will probably permit you to run many more programs. It all depends on how much of an investment you want to make.

2. Are the audio and visual presentations appealing?

Computer games have come a long way since they were first introduced. Don't settle for sloppy sound or uninteresting stick figures. (Then again, the quality of both the sound and the graphics will depend on what your computer is capable of handling. Full-color animated programs require fairly sophisticated hardware. Programs that generate complicated sounds — for example, music programs that play chords — require computers with fairly sophisticated "voice chips" built in. If all your computer can do is "beep," don't expect it to play Beethoven's Fifth.)

3. Is information presented speedily, or is there a great deal of waiting time between on-screen statements or instructions?

This, too, may depend on your computer. Generally speaking, the more internal memory a computer has, the faster programs will run. Computers with limited internal memory are naturally slower — and may not be able to run some programs at all.

4. Does the game give "feedback" about errors so my child can learn from his or her mistakes?

This feedback may be as simple as an on-screen statement saying "Good work!" or "Try again!" — or as complicated as animated figures jumping up and down to music and cheers. Optimally, the feedback will provide some clues when errors are made.

5. After my child quits the program for a while, is it possible to return quickly to where he or she left off earlier — or is it necessary to restart the program from the beginning?

Having to start over again wastes time. It's also boring to repeat the same steps one has already done successfully.

Following are titles and brief descriptions of several computer games that meet our standards of suitability for children. Please note that this list is up-to-date as of September, 1988. Computer programs are continually being revised and changed, and new ones are put on the market regularly. For information about new programs, read reviews in current issues of publications like those named on page 113. See pages 117 - 118 for manufacturers' addresses in the event that you can't find specific games in stores.

▶ **Reading Programs**

- *Ace Reporter* (MindPlay). Users answer "who-what-when-where-why-how" questions to meet "article deadlines." For intermediate students. (Apple)

- *Bouncy Bee Learns Words* (IBM). Tutors and provides games for 250 high-frequency words; comes with read-aloud stories. For primary students. (IBM)

- *Fact or Opinion* (Hartley Courseware). Teaches the differences between facts and opinions. (Apple, IBM)

- *Gapper/Gapper Anthology* (HRM Software). Combines word processing with timed reading, multiple choice, and fill-in-the-blank activities for stories of some length. For intermediate students. (Apple)

- *Kermit's Electronic Storymaker* (Simon & Schuster). Users select phrases to put together into animated sentences. (Apple, Commodore)

- *M SS NG L NKS: Young People's Literature* (Sunburst). Provides fill-in-the-blank activities using passages from children's literature. For intermediate students. (Apple, Atari, Commodore, IBM)

- *The Puzzler* (Sunburst). Users make and test predictions in mysteries. For intermediate students. (Apple, Commodore, IBM)

- *Reading for Information* (for content material) and *Reading for Meaning* (for stories; both IBM). Each teaches reading comprehension. (IBM)

- *Rhyme 'N Read* (SVE). Provides practice in rhyming words in illustrated stories. (Apple)

- *Semantic Mapper* (Teacher Support Software). Provides practice in vocabulary from the basal reader or other sources. For intermediate students. (Apple)

- *Stickybear Reading* (Weekly Reader Family Software). Provides practice in illustrated word recognition and sentence structure. For younger children. (Apple, Commodore)

- *Tales of Discovery* (Scholastic). Provides problem-solving adventure stories. For intermediate students. (Apple, Commodore, IBM)

- *Those Amazing Reading Machines* (MECC). Provides practice with detail and sequence as users match sequences of actions with pictures of machines. For intermediate students. (Apple)

▶ **Spelling and Writing Programs**

- *Crossword Magic* (Mindscape). Creates crossword puzzles out of user-supplied vocabulary words and definitions. (Apple, Atari, Commodore, IBM)

- *Explore-a-Story* (Collamore Heath). Users can change graphics and backgrounds while working with a simple word processing program; comes with storybooks. For primary and intermediate students. (Apple)

- *Story Starter* (Random House). Teaches cause-and-effect and sequence as users write stories. (Apple)

- *Storyteller* (Educational Activities). Users read or create stories. For intermediate students. (Apple, IBM)

- *Suspect Sentences* (Silver Burdett & Ginn). A "forger" (player 1) inserts a sentence into a paragraph so it cannot be detected by a "detective" (player 2). To be good forgers, students must attend to capitalization, punctuation, sentence structure, spelling, and style. For intermediate students. (Apple)

- *Tiger's Tales* (Sunburst). Users match words and sentences with pictures to produce simple stories. For younger children. (Apple, Commodore)

- *Word Wizards* (MECC). Turns vocabulary and spelling lists into practice activities. (Apple)

- *Writer Rabbit* (Learning Co.) Tutors and provides games for "who-what-where-when-why" questions. For younger children. (Apple, Tandy, IBM)

NOTE: For information on word processing programs, see pages 7 - 9.

▶ **Math Programs**

- *Conquering Whole Numbers* (MECC). Provides practice in addition, subtraction, multiplication, and division; includes three strategy games. For intermediate students. (Apple)

- *Learning Place Value* (Mindscape). Teaches estimation and place value. (Apple, IBM, Tandy)

- *Math Rabbit* (Learning Co.) Explores counting and other basic number concepts. For younger children. (Apple, IBM)

- *Number Stumper* (Learning Co.) Four games provide practice in addition and subtraction. For primary and intermediate students. (Apple)

- *WordMath* (intermediate) and *Primary WordMath* (Milliken). Teaches users how to solve word problems. (Apple)

▶ **Other Programs**

- *Surveys Unlimited: A Tool for Survey Takers* (Mindscape). Users create, print, and administer surveys. Data can be analyzed in line, bar, or pie graphs. For intermediate students. (Apple)

- *Where in the USA is Carmen SanDiego, Where in Europe is Carmen SanDiego, and Where in the World is Carmen SanDiego* (Broderbund). Teaches geography as users solve "whodunits" with the help of almanacs supplied with the program. For intermediate students. (Apple)

ADDRESSES FOR MAKERS OF RECOMMENDED GAMES

If you can't find games of interest in stores or catalogs, you can write the manufacturers. In some cases, you can order directly from the manufacturer (after requesting order information). In other cases, the manufacturer will refer you to stores in your area that carry their products.

As long as you're writing, request a catalog, too. You may find descriptions of other games that may be worth considering.

Broderbund
17 Paul Drive
San Rafael, CA 94903

Cardinal Industries
201 51st Ave.
Long Island City, NY 11101

Coleco Games
999 Quaker Lane South
W. Hartford, CT 06110

Collamore Heath
125 Spring St.
Lexington, MA 02173

DLM Teaching Resources
One DLM Park
Allen, TX 75002

Educational Activities
PO Box 392
Freeport, NY 11520

Frank Schaffer Publications
19771 Magellan Drive
Torrance, CA 90202

Hartley Courseware
PO Box 431
Dimondale, MI 48821

HRM Software
175 Tompkins Ave.
Pleasantville, NY 10570

IBM
PO Box 1328
Boca Raton, FL 33432

(continued on next page)

Learning Co.
545 Middlefield Rd., #170
Menlo Park, CA 94025

MECC (Minnesota Educational
    Computer Consortium)
3490 Lexington Ave. North
St. Paul MN 55126-8097

Milliken Publishing Co.
1100 Research Blvd.
PO Box 21579
St. Louis, MO 63132-0579

Milton Bradley Company
PO Box 3400
Springfield, MA 01101

MindPlay
82 Montvale Ave.
Stone, MA 02180

Mindscape
3444 Dundee Rd.
Northbrook, IL 60062

Parker Brothers
50 Dunham Rd.
Beverly, MA 01915

Pressman Toy Co.
200 5th Ave.
New York, NY

Random House
School Division
400 Hahn Road
Westminster, MD 21157

Scholastic
730 Broadway
New York, NY 10003

Silver Burdett & Ginn
250 James St.
Morristown, NJ 07960

Sunburst Communications
39 Washington Ave.
Pleasantville, NY 10570-9971

SVE
Dept. 333
Danbury, CT 06186

Teacher Support Software
PO Box 7130
Gainesville, FL 32605-7130

Weekly Reader Family Software
PO Box 16618
Columbus, OH 4321

Games you can make yourself

When the cost of a commercial game is prohibitive or unwarranted, when a commercial game is not readily available for a specific skill your child needs to master, or when you decide at the spur of the moment that an educational game would liven up a homework session — then make one yourself! Here are some general guidelines for creating homemade learning games:

▶ Don't spend more time making the game than your child will spend playing it. (Depending on the skill it's intended to teach, you may only need to use it once or twice.)

▶ Have a specific learning goal in mind. Don't try to incorporate too many goals into one game.

▶ Get your child involved in the game-making process. You may want to turn this into a problem-solving activity. ("Let's see, you need to study your states and capitals. How can we make a game of it?")

▶ Brainstorm together an imaginative name or theme for the game.

▶ Have plenty of materials on hand — scissors, construction paper, cardboard, markers, rulers, and so on. If neither you nor your child is artistically inclined, use magazine, comic book, or coloring book pictures to decorate the game. Stickers and rubber stamps are other creative possibilities.

▶ WRITE THE RULES DOWN. Not only does this avoid future conflict; it also models a writing activity for your child.

▶ Don't feel as if you have to make game cards for each and every game. For example, if your child needs to prepare for a science test, just use the questions at the end of the chapter or make up questions based on the text. If your child needs to drill on math problems or reading exercises, use the problems or exercises from the text.

▶ Finally, store all learning games and game pieces in the study center. Use a plastic dishwashing tub, a milk crate, a tote bag, or a special shelf for keeping all the odds and ends together.

Recommended game formats and suggested applications

This section provides some "generic" game formats you can adapt to your child's interests and tailor to skills that need reinforcing. Use your imagination (and your child's) to build these into enjoyable games that meet educational goals. These formats are appropriate for elementary children of all ages; the level of difficulty depends on the content.

We have suggested applications for each format. Many applications are interchangeable from format to format.

We have also provided sample "cards" or "boards" for some games on pages 187 - 191. TIP: Photocopy several of these pages, then cut out the cards or boards and have them laminated (or cover them with clear contact paper) so they can be written on with erasable crayon and used several times. Naturally you can also use paper and pencil or chalkboard and chalk for most of these games.

BINGO

Materials needed:

▶ Poker chips, pennies, or squares of paper for space markers

▶ Traditional five-column BINGO cards (see page 187)

▶ BINGO numbers

Rules of play:

1. Call out a question or flash a flashcard.

2. If your child provides the correct response, draw a BINGO number, call it out, and have your child put a marker on the corresponding space.

3. Play continues until your child gets "BINGO" — five markers in a row either horizontally, vertically, or diagonally.

Sample applications:

▶ LEARNING LETTERS: Write lower-case letters on the BINGO card. Make flashcards of corresponding upper-case letters. (Or do this the other way around.) Show your child a flashcard and ask him or her to match it to a letter on the BINGO board. *Variation*: Have your child match cursive with manuscript letters.

▶ LEARNING VOWELS: Label the 5 columns on the board with A-E-I-O-U rather than B-I-N-G-O. Call out a word. If your child correctly identifies the vowel sound, he or she may place a marker in any square in that vowel column.

▶ LEARNING SIGHT WORDS: Write vocabulary words in the squares on the BINGO board. Read them aloud, one at a time, and have your child cover each word he or she recognizes.

▶ LEARNING MATH FACTS: Write numerals and math symbols in the squares on the BINGO card. Call out the numbers or symbols ("one," "plus," "divided by") and have your child cover each one he or she recognizes.

▶ STUDYING SCIENCE OR SOCIAL STUDIES QUESTIONS: Write answers on the BINGO board. Read the questions and have your child cover each match.

▶ LEARNING STATES AND CAPITALS: Call out a capital. If your child correctly names the state, draw a BINGO number card and have your child cover the corresponding square on the card. (Or do this the other way around: you name the state, and your child names the capital.)

TIC-TAC-TOE

Materials needed:

▶ Tic-tac-toe board (see page 189)

Rules of play:

1. Your child is "X" and you're "O."

2. Ask your child a question. If your child answers it correctly, he or she places an "X" on the board. If your child answers it incorrectly, you place an "O" on the board.

3. Play continues until one of you gets "TIC-TAC-TOE" — three X's or O's in a row either horizontally, vertically, or diagonally.

Sample applications:

▶ LEARNING VOCABULARY: Have your child define vocabulary terms.

▶ LEARNING GRAMMAR: Have your child complete an item in a grammar exercise (for example, locate a subject or verb in a sentence).

▶ LEARNING COUNTING: "Skip count" by 2's, 3's, or 4's (or some other number) up to a certain number, then have your child give the next number in the sequence.

▶ LEARNING SPELLING: Dictate a spelling word, then have your child write it correctly.

DOTS GAME

Materials needed:

▶ Dots board (see page 191)

Rules of play:

1. Explain that the object of the game is to make squares by joining dots with horizontal and vertical lines.

2. Ask your child a question. If your child answers it correctly, he or she draws a line on the board. If your child answers it incorrectly, you draw a line on the board.

3. When a square is completed, the player puts his or her initials inside the box and immediately gets another turn.

4. When all squares on the board have been completed, the player with the most initialed squares wins.

Sample applications:

▶ LEARNING CONSONANTS: Read a word out loud. Have your child identify the beginning or ending consonant sound.

▶ LEARNING PREFIXES OR SUFFIXES: Show your child a word written on a flashcard. Have him or her identify the prefix or suffix.

▶ LEARNING CAPITALIZATION AND PUNCTUATION: Show your child a sentence with a capitalization or punctuation error. Have him or her identify the error and explain how it should be corrected.

▶ LEARNING ROMAN NUMERALS: Show your child Roman numerals written on flashcards, and have him or her identify them.

▶ LEARNING TO READ MAPS OR GRAPHICS: Ask questions about maps or graphics you show to your child.

CONCENTRATION

Materials needed:

▶ Flashcards or playing cards with word or math problems written on one side. Each card must have a match — either a duplicate of the problem, or the answer to the problem.

The difficulty of the game will depend on the problems themselves and the number of cards used.

Rules of play:

1. Shuffle the cards, then lay them out one deep and upside-down in a square or a rectangle.

2. To take a turn, a player turns any two cards up.

3. If the cards match, the player removes them from the board and immediately gets another turn.

4. If the cards don't match, the next player takes a turn.

5. Play continues until all matches have been made. The player with the most matches wins.

Sample applications:

▶ LEARNING SIGHT WORDS: Make card sets using vocabulary words. Have your child say the word out loud when he or she finds a match.

▶ LEARNING SYNONYMS *(big-large)*, ANTONYMS *(big-small)*, AND HOMONYMS *(blue-blew)*: Make card sets using these kinds of words.

▶ LEARNING MATH FACTS: Make card sets of math problems having the same answer (for example, "1 + 5" and "4 + 2," or "6 x 2" and "3 x 4").

▶ LEARNING THE PARTS OF SPEECH: Make card sets of examples and definitions.

▶ LEARNING MAP SYMBOLS: Make card sets of map symbols or abbreviations and definitions.

CARD GAMES

Materials needed:

▶ Homemade playing cards with words or math problems on one side. Each card must have a match — either a duplicate of the problem, or the answer.

Rules of play:

Follow the rules for "Go Fish" or "Wet Cat" (played the same as "Old Maid"). In the case of "Wet Cat," a wildcard will be needed.

Sample applications:

▶ rhyming words

▶ the halves of compound words

▶ vocabulary words and definitions

▶ words and their abbreviations

▶ Arabic and Roman numerals

HANGMAN

Materials needed:

▶ Paper and pencil, or chalkboard and chalk.

Rules of play:

1. Explain that the object of the game is to identify an unknown word, starting with only the number of letters.

2. Think of a word, then draw a space for each letter on the paper or chalkboard.

3. Have your child guess one letter at a time. If the letter is included in the "mystery word," write it in the appropriate blank space (or spaces). If the letter is not included in the word, draw a body part on the Hangman. (HINT: It's wise to agree ahead of time on which body parts should be included. Sometimes, in an attempt to win, children will want everything to count, from eyelashes to toenails.)

4. To win, your child must identify the mystery word before all the Hangman's body parts are drawn.

Sample applications:

▶ LEARNING SPELLING WORDS: Work from your child's test list for that week, and include review words from past weeks.

▶ LEARNING VOCABULARY WORDS: Have your child define the word after identifying it.

▶ LEARNING NAMES OF CITIES, STATES, COUNTRIES: Work from the chapters your child is studying in his or her social studies text, and include review names from past weeks.

MATCH-UPS

Several different formats can be used for matching games. Each requires a different set of materials, but all share the same rules and applications.

Materials needed for a Matching Wheel:

▶ Cut out a 14" circular piece of cardboard and draw lines dividing it into "pie pieces"

▶ Cover the cardboard with clear contact paper

▶ Use erasable crayon to label each pie piece with one-half of a match

▶ Use Post-It notes or clothespins to create the other halves of the matches (see illustration below)

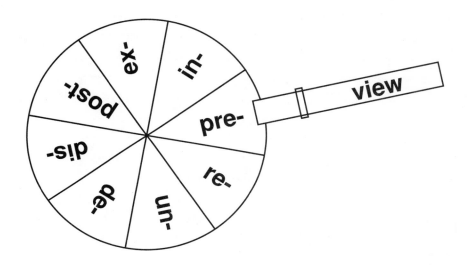

Materials needed for Matching Mini-Puzzles:

▶ Write one-half of a match on each side of an index card.

▶ Cut the card into two interlocking pieces.

Materials needed for Homemade Dominoes:

▶ Divide 2 x 4" pieces of tagboard in two by drawing a line down the middle of each one.

▶ On each half, draw a word, symbol, or number.

▶ Make sure that each word, symbol, or number is paired with itself at least once and paired with every other word, symbol, or number in the set at least once. Also make sure to include some blanks. Here's an example of what part of a set might look like:

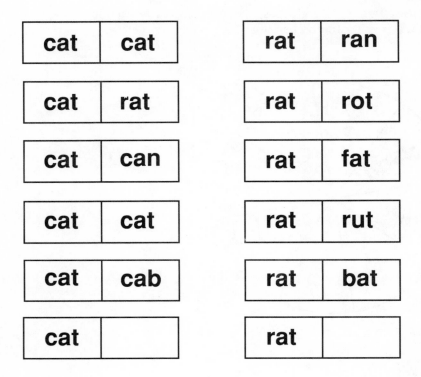

Rules of play, all Match-Up games:

Explain that the object of the game is simply to make all the matches correctly, reading them as they are made.

To add an element of excitement, have your child do this under timed conditions and try to better his or her time with each round.

Sample applications:

The applications for match-up games are virtually limitless. Types of matches might include:

▶ words and pictures representing the words

▶ prefixes or suffixes and root words

▶ names of landforms ("plateau," "peninsula") or bodies of water ("lake," "inlet") and diagrams or descriptions

▶ sentences with missing vocabulary words and the vocabulary words

▶ numerals and corresponding numbers of dots

▶ states and abbreviations

▶ measurement abbreviations and identifications

SORTING GAMES

Materials needed:

▶ Small slips of paper labeled with the names, problems, definitions, questions, etc. to be sorted

▶ Shoe boxes or small paper lunch bags, labeled and used as containers (for sorting only a few categories)

▶ Egg cartons (for sorting up to 12 different categories)

Rules of play:

Explain that the object of the game is simply to sort the items correctly into categories.

To add an element of excitement, have your child do this under timed conditions and try to better his or her time with each round.

Applications:

The applications for sorting games are virtually limitless. Categories might include:

▶ long and short vowel sounds

▶ hard and soft "g" and "c" words (*go* and *age*, *cat* and *face*)

▶ true and false statements

▶ animals (vertebrates or invertebrates, warm-blooded or cold-blooded)

▶ singular and plural nouns

Making your own board games

You don't have to make board games from scratch to create ones that meet your goals for your child. You can use games you already have if you tie taking turns to answering questions, reading vocabulary words, or solving math problems. It's easy to design your own "Reading Pursuit," "Math Pursuit," "Spelling Pursuit," "Social Studies Pursuit," or whatever.

If you don't have any board games that you think will work for these purposes, here are some ideas to try:

▶ Folders from drugstores or discount stores (or office supplies stores) are great for board games. If the folder has a picture on the outside, it can help determine the theme of the game. For example, a folder with a baseball pitcher on the front can become "Syllable Strike-Out," and a folder with cats on the front can become "Capitalization Cat-Nap." Most folders are blank on the inside. Use this blank surface as the game board. Draw a path with crayons or felt-tipped pens, and be sure to include squares with instructions such as START, GO BACK (1, 2, 3) SPACES, GO FORWARD (1, 2, 3) SPACES, FREE TURN, FINISH, and so on. If the folder has a pocket, use it for storing place markers, rules, game pieces, scorepads, and other materials used to play the game.

▶ If your child is a sports fan, draw a football, soccer, or baseball field instead of a regular game board pathway. Your child earns "yardage," "goals," or "base hits" with every correct answer.

▶ Instead of making a traditional square or rectangular game board, cut it in the shape of a favorite cartoon character; a musical instrument; a state, country, or continent; a car or locomotive; and so on.

▶ Science board games can be especially interesting. The path you draw might wind through the human circulatory or digestive system, the solar system, or layers of the earth (from core to crust) — with these serving as the game themes.

▶ Real road maps make excellent game boards, and your child can learn map reading skills simultaneously. If your child is studying a country or a continent in social studies, try to find a map of the place he or she is studying. Use a felt-tipped pen to draw a pathway between major locations on a city, state, or country map.

▶ Instead of a board, why not use a yard stick or meter stick? With each correct answer, your child can move the marker (a slider or a rubber band) an inch or a decimeter.

You can use homemade board games to test almost anything — from sight words to math facts, spelling words to scientific concepts.

RESOURCES FOR MORE
MAKE-IT-YOURSELF GAMES

These books either contain learning games designed to satisfy specific objectives or tell you how to make them yourself. Since they may be hard to find in bookstores, we have included the publishers' addresses. If you are interested in adding one or more to your home library, write to the publisher(s) or ask your bookstore to order copies for you. Many bookstores do special ordering as a service to their customers.

Bell, Irene Wood and Weickert, Jeanne E. *Basic Media Skills through Games* (Libraries Unlimited, Inc., 1985). ADDRESS: PO Box 263, Littleton, CO 80160.

Forgan, Harry W. *The Reading Corner* (Scott, Foresman & Company, 1977) and Forgan, Harry W. and Striebel, Bonnie, *Phorgan's Phonics* (1978). ADDRESS: 1900 E. Lake Ave., Glenview, IL 60025.

Graves, Ruth, editor. *Reading Is Fundamental Guide to Encouraging Young Readers* (Doubleday and Co., Inc., 1987). ADDRESS: 245 Park Ave., New York, NY 10017.

Hanson, Jeanne K. *Game Plans for Children* (G.P. Putnam's Sons, 1982). ADDRESS: 200 Madison Ave., New York, NY 10016.

Kaye, Peggy. *Games for Math* (Pantheon Press, 1987) and *Games for Reading* (1984). ADDRESS: 201 E. 50th St., New York, NY 10022.

9

Resources and Tools for Parents

"Read, not to contract and confute; not to believe and take for granted; not to find talk and discourse; but to weigh and consider."
— Francis Bacon

Books for Parents

These books contain additional information for caring parents. Since they may be hard to find in bookstores, we have included the publishers' addresses.

Albert, Linda. *Coping with Kids and School* (E.P. Dutton, 1985). ADDRESS: 2 Park Ave., New York, NY 10016. Easy-to-read questions and answers to school-related problems.

Greene, Lawrence J. *Kids Who Hate School* (Fawcett, 1987). ADDRESS: Fawcett, A Division of Ballantine Books, Random House, 201 E. 50th St., New York, NY 10022. Written by a learning disabilities specialist, this book presents case histories which deal with all aspects of parenting the learning-disabled child.

Hartmann, Donna and Stump, Arlyss. *Your Child Can Read Better: A Handbook for Parents* (Learning Publications, Inc., 1980). ADDRESS: Box 1326, Dept. C., Holmes Beach, FL 33509. Background information about reading, with after-school and summer reading activities, games, and gift ideas.

Hearne, Betsy. *Choosing Books for Children: A Commonsense Guide* (Dell, 1982). ADDRESS: 1 Dag Hammarskjold Plaza, 245 E. 47th St., New York, NY 10017. Chapters are devoted to selecting different types of books; over 100 titles are recommended.

Kimmel, Margaret M. and Segal, Elizabeth. *For Reading Out Loud!* (Delacorte, 1983). ADDRESS: 1 Dag Hammarskjold Plaza, New York, NY 10017. Explains why it's important to read aloud all through the childhood years; tells how to make time to do it; and gives effective ways of reading over 140 suggested books.

Lamme, Linda Leonard. *Highlights for Children Growing Up Reading* (Acropolis Books, Ltd., 1985). ADDRESS: Colortone Building, 2400 17th St. N.W., Washington, D.C. 20009. Information about the development of language and reading skills, with activities for fostering reading appreciation and skills acquisition in the home.

Larrick, Nancy. *A Parent's Guide to Better Reading* (Westminster, 1983). ADDRESS: 925 Chestnut St., Philadelphia, PA 19107. Considered a classic; names favorite books and tells parents how to encourage reading at home.

Russell, William. *Classics to Read Aloud to Your Children* (Crown, 1984). ADDRESS: PO Box 117, Knob Noster, MO 65336. Each selection indicates the age of the child it is suited for and offers suggestions for making a read-aloud session enjoyable.

Saunders, Jacqulyn and Espeland, Pamela. *Bringing Out the Best: A Resource Guide for Parents of Young Gifted Children* (Free Spirit Publishing, 1986). ADDRESS: 123 North Third St., Suite 716, Minneapolis, MN 55401. Written by parents for parents, this book includes information ranging from ways to build a child's self-esteem to tips on dealing successfully with teachers and schools.

Trelease, Jim. *The Read-Aloud Handbook* (Penguin Books, 1985). ADDRESS: 40 W. 23rd St., New York, NY 10010. Discusses the hows and whys of reading aloud; contains over 300 annotated read-aloud selections.

More recommended reading for parents

The following publications are available for a nominal fee from the International Reading Association, 800 Barksdale Rd., PO Box 8139, Newark, DE 19714.

Baghban, Marcia. *How Can I Help My Child Learn to Read English as a Second Language?* (This publication has also been translated into Spanish by Ricardo L. Garcia and Rita Maxine Deyoe).

Chan, Julie M.T. *Why Read Aloud to Children?*

Eberly, Donald W. *How Does My Child's Vision Affect His Reading?*

Glazer, Susan Mandel. *How Can I Help My Child Build Positive Attitudes toward Reading?*

Ransbury, Molly Kayes. *How Can I Encourage My Primary Grade Child to Read?*

Rogers, Norma. *How Can I Help My Child Get Ready to Read?*, *What Books and Records Should I Get for My Preschooler?*, and *What Is Reading Readiness?*

Winebrenner, Rosemary. *How Can I Get My Teenager to Read?*

Additional resources

The following organizations are excellent sources of information for parents.

▶ American Library Association, 50 E. Huron St., Chicago, IL 60611.

Write to the ALA for lists of recommended books for children.

▶ International Reading Association, 800 Barksdale Rd., PO Box 8139, Newark, DE 19714.

Single copies of these brochures are available at no charge. When requesting copies, please enclose a self-addressed, stamped envelope:

- "Eating Well Can Help Your Child Learn Better"
- "Good Books Make Reading Fun for Your Child"
- "Summer Reading Is Important"

- "You Can Encourage Your Child to Read"
- "You Can Use Television to Stimulate Your Child's Reading Habits"
- "Your Home Is Your Child's First School"

▶ National Council for Teachers of English, Order Dept., 1111 Kenyon Road, Urbana, IL 61801.

Write for a copy of "How to Help Your Child Become a Better Writer."

▶ Reading Is Fundamental, Inc., Publications Department, 600 Maryland Ave. S.W., Washington, D.C. 20024.

Copies of these pamphlets are available on request:

- "Children Who Can Read, But Don't"
- "Choosing Good Books for Children"
- "TV and Reading"
- "Upbeat and Offbeat Activities to Encourage Reading"

Tools for parents

On the following pages you'll find forms, lists, charts, game boards, and more that can help you to help your child with homework. Suggestions for using them are included throughout the book, but don't limit yourself to these alone. You may find that some serve several purposes.

You will notice that we have included alternative versions of some of the forms. Let your child choose the one he or she likes best.

Permission is granted to reproduce any and all of the following pages for home and classroom use.

CERTIFICATE OF
CONGRATULATIONS

TO

DATE

For successfully completing

Good Job!

Keep It Up!

Good Work!

Signed

CERTIFICATE OF
CONGRATULATIONS

TO

_____

DATE

_____

For successfully completing

_____

Keep It Up!   **Good Job!**

**GOOD
WORK!**

_____
Signed

WEEK OF: _____

DATE OF ASSIGNMENT	SUBJECT	BOOK OR PROJECT	PAGE	DATE DUE	GRADE

Assignment Sheet

WEEK OF: _____

DATE OF ASSIGNMENT	SUBJECT	BOOK OR PROJECT	PAGE	DATE DUE	GRADE

THE INSTANT (SIGHT) WORDS

Edward Fry

THE FIRST 100 WORDS (approximately first grade)

Group 1a	Group 1b	Group 1c	Group 1d
the	he	go	who
a	I	see	an
is	they	then	their
you	one	us	she
to	good	no	new
and	me	him	said
we	about	by	did
that	had	was	boy
in	if	come	three
not	some	get	down
for	up	or	work
at	her	two	put
with	do	man	were
it	when	little	before
on	so	has	just
can	my	them	long
will	very	how	here
are	all	like	other
of	would	our	old
this	any	what	take
your	been	know	cat
as	out	make	again
but	there	which	give
be	from	much	after
have	day	his	many

THE INSTANT (SIGHT) WORDS

Edward Fry

THE SECOND 100 WORDS (approximately second grade)

Group 2a	Group 2b	Group 2c	Group 2d
saw	big	may	ran
home	where	let	five
soon	am	use	read
stand	ball	these	over
box	morning	right	such
upon	live	present	way
first	four	tell	too
came	last	next	shall
girl	color	please	own
house	away	leave	most
find	red	hand	sure
because	friend	more	thing
made	pretty	why	only
could	eat	better	near
book	want	under	than
look	year	while	open
mother	white	should	kind
run	got	never	must
school	play	each	high
people	found	best	far
night	left	another	both
into	men	seem	end
say	bring	tree	also
think	wish	name	until
back	black	dear	call

THE INSTANT (SIGHT) WORDS

Edward Fry

THE THIRD 100 WORDS (approximately third grade)

Group 3a	Group 3b	Group 3c	Group 3d
ask	hat	off	fire
small	car	sister	ten
yellow	write	happy	order
show	try	once	part
goes	myself	didn't	early
clean	longer	set	fat
buy	those	round	third
thank	hold	dress	same
sleep	full	fell	love
letter	carry	wash	hear
jump	eight	start	yesterday
help	sing	always	eyes
fly	warm	anything	door
don't	sit	around	clothes
fast	dog	close	through
cold	ride	walk	o'clock
today	hot	money	second
does	grow	turn	water
face	cut	might	town
green	seven	hard	took
every	woman	along	pair
brown	funny	bed	now
coat	yes	fine	keep
six	ate	sat	head
gave	stop	hope	food

THE INSTANT (SIGHT) WORDS

Edward Fry

THE SECOND 300 WORDS (approximately fourth grade)

Group 4a	Group 4b	Group 4c	Group 4d
told	time	word	wear
Miss	yet	almost	Mr.
father	true	thought	side
children	above	send	poor
land	still	receive	lost
interest	meet	pay	outside
government	since	nothing	wind
feet	number	need	Mrs.
garden	state	mean	learn
done	matter	late	held
country	line	half	front
different	remember	fight	built
bad	large	enough	family
across	few	feel	began
yard	hit	during	air
winter	cover	gone	young
table	window	hundred	ago
story	even	week	world
sometimes	city	between	airplane
I'm	together	change	without
tried	sun	being	kill
horse	life	care	ready
something	street	answer	stay
brought	party	course	won't
shoes	suit	against	paper

THE INSTANT (SIGHT) WORDS

Edward Fry

THE SECOND 300 WORDS (continued)

Group 4e	Group 4f	Group 4g	Group 4h
hour	grade	egg	spell
glad	brother	ground	beautiful
follow	remain	afternoon	sick
company	milk	feed	became
believe	several	boat	cry
begin	war	plan	finish
mind	able	question	catch
pass	charge	fish	floor
reach	either	return	stick
month	less	sir	great
point	train	fell	guess
rest	cost	hill	bridges
sent	evening	wood	church
talk	note	add	lady
went	past	ice	tomorrow
bank	room	chair	snow
ship	flew	watch	whom
business	office	alone	women
whole	cow	low	among
short	visit	arm	road
certain	wait	dinner	farm
fair	teacher	hair	cousin
reason	spring	service	bread
summer	picture	class	wrong
fill	bird	quite	age

THE INSTANT (SIGHT) WORDS

Edward Fry

THE SECOND 300 WORDS (continued)

Group 4i	Group 4j	Group 4k	Group 4l
become	herself	demand	aunt
body	idea	however	system
chance	drop	figure	lie
act	river	case	cause
die	smile	increase	marry
real	son	enjoy	possible
speak	bat	rather	supply
already	fact	sound	thousand
doctor	sort	eleven	pen
step	king	music	condition
itself	dark	human	perhaps
nine	themselves	court	produce
baby	whose	force	twelve
minute	study	plant	rode
ring	fear	suppose	uncle
wrote	move	law	labor
happen	stood	husband	public
appear	himself	moment	consider
heart	strong	person	thus
swim	knew	result	least
felt	often	continue	power
fourth	toward	price	mark
I'll	wonder	serve	president
kept	twenty	national	voice
well	important	wife	whether

• STORY STUDY GUIDE •

How To Help Your Child With Homework, copyright © 1988 by Marguerite Radencich and Jeanne Schumm.

Title: _____

Author: _____

About the Setting

Time: _____

Place: _____

About the Characters

_____

_____

_____

_____

_____

About the Story

The major problem in the story: _____

_____

_____

_____

How the problem was resolved: _____

_____

_____

_____

About the Plot

_____

_____

_____

_____

Vocabulary

Identify and define the most difficult words in the story

_____

_____

_____

_____

Story
• STUDY GUIDE •

Title: _____

Author: _____

About the Setting

    Time _____

    Place _____

About the Characters
Give names and nicknames, physical descriptions,
personality descriptions

_____

_____

_____

_____

_____

_____

_____

_____

_____

About the Story
The major problem in the story: _____

_____

_____

_____

How the problem was resolved: _____

_____

_____

_____

About the Plot (list 5 major events in the story)

_____

_____

_____

_____

_____

Vocabulary
Identify and define the most difficult words in the story

_____

_____

_____

_____

MANUSCRIPT CHART
Zaner–Bloser Style

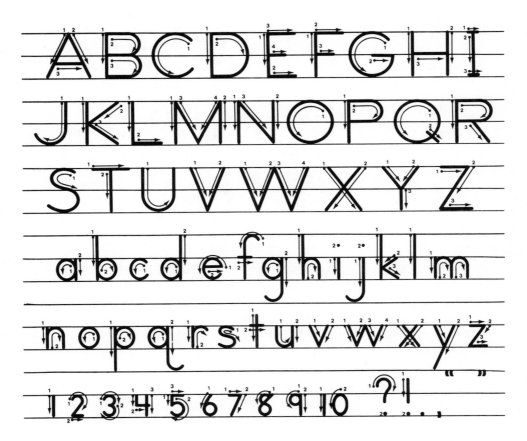

MANUSCRIPT CHART

D' Nealian Style

MANUSCRIPT PRACTICE PAPER

Cursive Chart
Zaner-Bloser

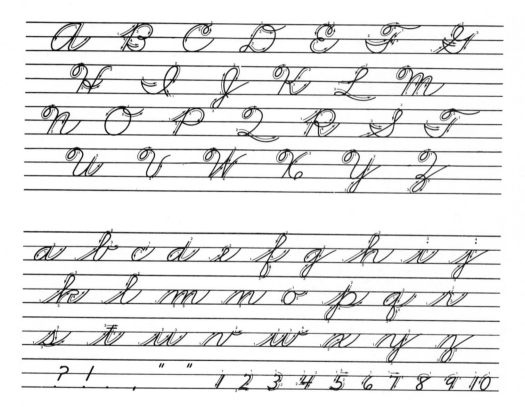

Cursive Practice—Sample

ate *tea* *lad* *bad*

dab *abe* *cat* *tad*

ace *day* *ade* *rod*

eat *pea* *tree* *fat*

life *if* *got* *dog*

age *kid* *ache* *oh*

it *hid* *ski* *jug*

kind *take* *book*

late *old* *hill* *mat*

comb dim hot end

am oat toe too pad

ape loop rail air

drum star ask last

tag art ate use

put out you fat

give with own hair

library hurt first year

eye many too funny

Cursive Practice Paper

+	0	1	2	3	4	5	6	7	8	9
0										
1										
2										
3										
4										
5										
6										
7										
8										
9										

XXX MULTIPLICATION TABLE XXX

X	0	1	2	3	4	5	6	7	8	9
0										
1										
2										
3										
4										
5										
6										
7										
8										
9										

SPECIAL
PROJECT CHECKLIST

STEP		DATE DONE

☐ 1. Decide on a project theme.   _____

☐ 2. Have theme approved by teacher.   _____

THEME: _____

☐ 3. Make a list of what needs to be done and the order in which the tasks should be completed. (List, then number each task.)

☐ 4. Decide who is going to do what. (Initial each task.)

☐ 5. Set deadlines for completion of each task. (Write in the dates.)

TASK	DATE DUE	DATE DONE	PERSON RESPONSIBLE
_____	_____	_____	_____
_____	_____	_____	_____
_____	_____	_____	_____
_____	_____	_____	_____
_____	_____	_____	_____
_____	_____	_____	_____
_____	_____	_____	_____

☐ 6. Make a list of materials needed to do the project. ☞

☐7. Make a projected budget. (Write the estimated cost of each item.)

ITEM   **COST**

_____

_____

_____

_____

☐8. Send away for resource materials needed.

RESOURCE MATERIAL   **DATE**   **DATE**
                                    REQUESTED   **RECEIVED**

_____

_____

_____

_____

☐9. Contact community resources.

COMMUNITY RESOURCE   **DATE CONTACTED**

_____

_____

_____

☐10. Visit the library.

PURPOSE OF VISIT   **DATE OF VISIT**

_____

_____

_____

☐11. Complete the project ON SCHEDULE.

DATE TURNED IN: _____ **GRADE:** _____

SPECIAL
PROJECT AGREEMENT
•FORM•

Today's Date: _____ Due Date: _____

Project Theme: _____

I, _____, agree to do the following tasks
       STUDENT'S NAME
by myself. I agree to do them on time.

TASK   **DATE DUE**

_____

_____

_____

I, _____ , and I, _____,
       PARENT'S NAME   STUDENT'S NAME
agree to do the following tasks together. We agree to do them
on time.

TASK   **DATE DUE**

_____

_____

_____

BOOK REPORT OUTLINE

I. INTRODUCTION

    A. Title of book: _____

    B. Author: _____

    C. Type of book (example: mystery, adventure, fantasy):

        _____

    D. Setting of book

        Time: _____

        Place: _____

    E. Why I read this book:

        _____

        _____

        _____

II. MAIN CHARACTERS

        _____

        _____

        _____

        _____

        _____

        _____

BOOK REPORT OUTLINE

III. SUMMARY OF BOOK

_____

_____

_____

_____

_____

IV. MY FEELINGS ABOUT THIS BOOK

A. The part I liked best:

_____

_____

_____

B. The part I liked least:

_____

_____

_____

C. This book was (check one)

_____ hard to read
_____ easy to read
_____ in between

D. I (check one)
_____ would
_____ would not
recommend this book to someone else because:

_____

_____

_____

BOOK REPORT OUTLINE

• FICTION BOOK •

I. INTRODUCTION
A. Title of book: _____
B. Author: _____
C. Type of book (example: mystery, adventure, fantasy):
_____
D. Setting of book
Time: _____
Place: _____
E. Why I read this book:
_____

II. CHARACTERS
A. Main character (name and description):
_____
B. Other important characters (names and descriptions):
_____
_____
_____
_____
_____

☞

BOOK REPORT OUTLINE

III. SUMMARY OF PLOT

_____

_____

_____

_____

_____

_____

_____

IV. CRITIQUE

   A. The part I liked best:

_____

_____

_____

   B. The part I liked least:

_____

_____

_____

   C. This book was (check one)

     _____ hard to read
     _____ easy to read
     _____ in between

   D. I (check one)
     _____ would
     _____ would not
   recommend this book to someone else because:

_____

_____

BOOK REPORT OUTLINE

I.   INTRODUCTION

    A.   Title of book: _____

    B.   Author: _____

    C.   Subject of book: _____

    D.   Why I read this book:

       _____

       _____

       _____

II.   SUMMARY OF BOOK

       _____

       _____

       _____

       _____

       _____

       _____

       _____

       _____

BOOK REPORT OUTLINE

III. NEW AND INTERESTING FACTS I LEARNED
FROM READING THIS BOOK

_____

_____

_____

_____

_____

IV. MY FEELINGS ABOUT THIS BOOK

    A.   The part I liked best:

_____

_____

_____

    B.   The part I liked least:

_____

_____

_____

    C.   This book was (check one)

       _____ hard to read
       _____ easy to read
       _____ in between

    D.   I (check one)
       _____ would
       _____ would not
    recommend this book to someone else because:

_____

_____

_____

BOOK REPORT OUTLINE
• NONFICTION BOOK •

I. INTRODUCTION

    A. Title of book: ―――――――――――――――――

    B. Author: ―――――――――――――――――――

    C. Subject of book: ―――――――――――――――

    D. Why I read this book:

    ――――――――――――――――――――――

    ――――――――――――――――――――――

    ――――――――――――――――――――――

    ――――――――――――――――――――――

II. SUMMARY OF BOOK

    ――――――――――――――――――――――

    ――――――――――――――――――――――

    ――――――――――――――――――――――

    ――――――――――――――――――――――

    ――――――――――――――――――――――

    ――――――――――――――――――――――

BOOK REPORT OUTLINE

III. NEW AND INTERESTING FACTS I LEARNED
FROM READING THIS BOOK

_____

_____

_____

_____

IV. CRITIQUE
   A. The part I liked best:

   _____

   _____

   _____

   B. The part I liked least:

   _____

   _____

   _____

   C. This book was (check one)

   _____ hard to read
   _____ easy to read
   _____ in between

   D. I (check one)
   _____ would
   _____ would not
   recommend this book to someone else because:

   _____

   _____

   _____

BIOGRAPHY

BOOK REPORT OUTLINE

How To Help Your Child With Homework, copyright © 1988 by Marguerite Radencich and Jeanne Schumm.

I. INTRODUCTION

    A. Title of book: _____

    B. Author: _____

    C. Who the book was about:

    _____

    _____

    D. Why I read this book:

    _____

    _____

    _____

    _____

II. WHAT I LEARNED ABOUT THIS PERSON

_____

_____

_____

_____

_____

_____

BOOK REPORT OUTLINE

III. WHY THIS PERSON IS REMEMBERED
OR ADMIRED TODAY

_____

_____

_____

_____

IV. MY FEELINGS ABOUT THIS BOOK

A. The part I liked best:

_____

_____

_____

B. The part I liked least:

_____

_____

_____

C. This book was (check one)

_____ hard to read
_____ easy to read
_____ in between

D. I (check one)
_____ would
_____ would not
recommend this book to someone else because:

_____

_____

_____

BOOK REPORT OUTLINE
• BIOGRAPHY BOOK •

I.   INTRODUCTION

    A.   Title of book: ————————————————————

    B.   Author: ——————————————————————

    C.   Subject of book: ——————————————————

    D.   Why I read this book:

        ————————————————————————

        ————————————————————————

        ————————————————————————

II. SUMMARY OF BOOK

    A.   What I learned about the person's life:

        ————————————————————————

        ————————————————————————

        ————————————————————————

    B.   What I learned about the person's major achievements:

        ————————————————————————

        ————————————————————————

        ————————————————————————

BOOK REPORT OUTLINE

III. PROBLEMS

    A.   The major problem in the person's life was:

    _____

    _____

    B.   Here is how this problem was solved:

    _____

    _____

IV. WHY THIS PERSON IS REMEMBERED
     OR ADMIRED TODAY

    _____

    _____

IV. CRITIQUE

    A.   The part I liked best:

    _____

    _____

    B.   The part I liked least:

    _____

    _____

    C.   This book was (check one)

          _____ hard to read
          _____ easy to read
          _____ in between

    D. I (check one)
          _____ would
          _____ would not
     recommend this book to someone else because:

    _____

    _____

TERM PAPER  CHECKLIST

ASSIGNMENT: To write a term paper on ——————————————

————————————————————————————————————

DATE DUE: ——————————————

REQUIREMENTS:
My paper will need:

☐   a title page
☐   a table of contents
☐   a bibliography
☐   graphics
    What kinds of graphics? ————————————————

It should be

☐   typed
☐   handwritten

STEP:		**DATE DUE**	**DATE DONE**
☐ 1.	Choose a topic	———	———
☐ 2.	Have topic approved by teacher	———	———
☐ 3.	Do library research	———	———
	———————————	———	———
	———————————	———	———
	———————————	———	———
☐ 4.	Contact community resources for information		

NAME OF RESOURCE:

———————————	———	———
———————————	———	———
———————————	———	———
———————————	———	———
———————————	———	———

TERM PAPER CHECKLIST

☐ 5. Write letters to obtain information
from national sources

WROTE LETTERS TO

	DATE DUE	DATE DONE
_____	_____	_____
_____	_____	_____
_____	_____	_____
_____	_____	_____

☐ 6. Take notes

TOOK NOTES FROM THESE SOURCES

_____	_____	_____
_____	_____	_____
_____	_____	_____
_____	_____	_____
_____	_____	_____
_____	_____	_____

☐ 7. Do an outline _____ _____

☐ 8. Write a rough draft _____ _____

☐ 9. Proofread rough draft; make corrections _____ _____

☐ 10. Write final draft _____ _____

☐ 11. Turn final draft in to teacher _____ _____

BINGO GAME CARDS

	B	I	N	G	O
1					
2					
3			FREE		
4					
5					

			FREE		

TIC TAC TOE BOARDS

DOTS GAME BOARDS

INDEX

About The Authors

Marguerite C. Radencich, Ph.D., is the K-Adult Reading Supervisor for Dade County Public Schools, Miami, Florida and an adjunct professor at several universities. She has published numerous professional articles and is coauthor with Dr. Gloria Kuchinskas of *The Semantic Mapper*, a vocabulary development program published by Teacher Support Software.

Jeanne Shay Schumm, Ph.D., is an Assistant Professor at the University of Miami. She coordinates their developmental reading program, and also writes professional articles about reading and study skills.